The Little Lights of Kimberley

And Other Plays

Harry Austin

A SAMUEL FRENCH ACTING EDITION

SAMUEL FRENCH

FOUNDED 1830

SAMUELFRENCH-LONDON.CO.UK
SAMUELFRENCH.COM

FOR AMATEUR PRODUCTION ENQUIRIES

UNITED KINGDOM AND WORLD EXCLUDING NORTH AMERICA
plays@SamuelFrench-London.co.uk
020 7255 4302/01

Each title is subject to availability from Samuel French,

depending upon country of performance.

CONTENTS

Following the success of Harry Austin's *The Chinese Pendant and Other Plays*, here are four more short plays, set in Victorian/Edwardian era. Easy to stage, with the minimum of scenery and properties, these playlets should prove very popular whenever light-hearted entertainment is called for.

The Little Lights of Kimberley

A heart-warming tale of how young war widow Lulu Littlehampton is saved from the dishonourable designs of Captain Harvey Kneetrembler and Arkwright, the Pickled Onion King, by the timely return of her husband Walter, who is not only not dead, but also very rich, having stumbled upon a hidden diamond mine!

The Green Eye of the Little Yellow Dog

A stirring tale of true love, devotion to duty and stark staring stupidity on the part of Captain Quincey Hogg, newly arrived adjutant at the British fort just north of Katmandu, who falls foul of the curse of the green eye of the little yellow dog.

The Brave Bugler or Up the Khyber Pass

Spurred on by the voluptuous Daphne, the diminutive but brave Bugler attempts to repulse single-handedly an attack on the British fort by marauding Indian tribesmen, only to lose Daphne to the suave officer who appears once the fighting is over.

Nellie's Nightlights

A Victorian/Edwardian comedy in which young Nellie Larkin becomes the "face that flickers in a thousand bedrooms", thanks to her invention of "Nellie's Nightlights".

THE LITTLE LIGHTS OF KIMBERLEY

A Victorian Comedy

CHARACTERS

Lulu, the young "war widow"
Sam Wormpit, her drunken father
Captain Harvey Kneetrembler, of the 29th Foot
Mr Arkwright, the Pickled Onion King
Walter Littlehampton, presumed missing

The action of the play takes place in a cottage living-room

Time—the 1890s

Running time approximately 16 minutes

THE LITTLE LIGHTS OF KIMBERLEY*

A sparsely furnished cottage living-room

There is an open fireplace upstage with a cradle standing in front. C, *a rickety table with a milk jug and a jam-jar of wild flowers on top, with one or two chairs by the table. A door leading into the street is* UL

As the CURTAIN *opens our heroine, Lulu Littlehampton, is rocking her baby in her arms. She walks down* L

Lulu Hush now, little Willie! Don't fret so! When Grandpa comes home I shall ask him to fetch a jug of fresh milk—that will comfort you! And Lord knows we shall need comforting these coming months. (*She picks up a buff paper telegram from the table*) Your poor father, reported missing from the war in Africa! Taken from us and not knowing he had a baby son! (*She sobs*) And me with only the clothes I stand up in and your poor old Grandpa, with no job and not a penny to bless his name with! (*She pats the baby and lies him carefully in the cradle*) Try and sleep a little, my angel! (*She moves* DL) I have to think about our future—if we have a future! (*She reads the telegram again, sobs and tucks it into the top of her dress*)

The door opens and her father, Sam Wormpit, enters. He is in his late fifties, wears a rumpled jacket and trousers, a shirt with detachable collar but no tie and has a battered bowler/derby type hat

Sam Lulu! Lulu! I got a *Chronicle*! (*He waves a newspaper*)
Lulu Over here, Father!
Sam Ah! There you are—you can read, Lulu, it might be about the war in Africa!

Lulu takes the newspaper and turns several pages

---

*N.B. Paragraph 3 on page ii of this Acting Edition regarding photocopying and video-recording should be carefully read.

Lulu Ah! Listen, Father. "Now that the native uprising has been quelled in M'Bongoland our brave soldiers of the Twenty-ninth Regiment of Foot have returned home as heroes. Sadly a few remain forever in Africa, a grim reminder of the savage fighting that took place to preserve the dignity of the British Empire. They shall not be forgotten." (*She lowers the newspaper and stares resolutely ahead, a break in her voice as she speaks*) Lance-Corporal Littlehampton will not be forgotten!

Sam (*placing his hat across his chest*) Ay! Young Walter were a good 'un. I wonder who will buy my beer now?

Lulu Beer? I am more concerned with finding money for food and keeping a roof over our heads! We are down to our last few coppers—we shall have to look for work!

Sam clutches his back in agony

Sam Ow! Ow! Ow! The stabbing pains!

Lulu Poor Father, I forgot about your lumbago—I must rub your back with liniment tonight!

She rubs his back and her father recovers

There is only one way—*I* shall have to go out after some money!

Sam You don't mean——?

Lulu Yes, I shall try for my old job in the pickle factory. Father, call on Mr Arkwright and ask him to find me a job—I will do anything!

Sam (*raising his eyebrows*) Old Arkwright will like that!

Lulu And on your way back, go to the diary and buy a wedge of cheese, a half a loaf and a jug of milk. (*She passes him the jug from the table*)

Sam What about money? I'm broke.

Lulu Here—take this ...

Lulu thrusts her hand into the top of her dress, fumbles and then drops a coin into Sam's hand. He passes the coin from hand to hand as it seems to be quite warm

That is our last sixpence—count the change!

Sam plants his hat firmly on his head, spits on the sixpence and goes off through the door

Lulu walks upstage to the cradle, rocks it

Not long to wait, little Willie. Grandpa will be back, then you shall have warm milk and we shall have bread and cheese—it could be our last meal for some time! (*She comes down front* L, *pulls out the telegram and reads it once more. She sobs and tucks it back*)

The door opens and in strides Captain Harvey Kneetrembler, resplendent in scarlet military uniform complete with cape over his shoulders and an impressive row of medals. He walks down front and turns L *to face Lulu*

Captain Beg pardon, ma'am! (*He clicks his heels, winces*)
Lulu (*startled*) Oh!
Captain Captain Harvey Kneetrembler. Twenty-ninth Regiment of Foot. At your service, ma'am. (*He smiles*) Are you Mrs Walter Littlehampton?
Lulu Yes! Yes, I am! Do you bring news of my husband—the Lance-Corporal?
Captain (*lowering his face*) Alas, ma'am. The only news I bring is—sad news, I'm afraid.
Lulu You haven't found my Walter then?
Captain We searched the battle area, ma'am. Not a sign of him.
Lulu Could he still be alive—a prisoner of war?
Captain A prisoner? (*He shakes his head*) He would have been hung by the "Fuzzy-Wuzzies"!
Lulu (*putting her hands to her face*) Oh, how painful for Walter! (*She sobs*)
Captain Bear up, ma'am! I bring a few personal items for you. This—your photograph, he kept it nailed to a tent pole. (*He reads*) "With love, from Lulu." (*He hands over the photograph. Speaking out front*) A right little Lulu, too! (*He strokes his moustache*) Also, to honour a brave soldier, this medal.

He removes the medal from its box and attempts to pin it to Lulu's chest. She proudly sticks her chest out, he dithers and fumbles

May I? It should go on the left—er, perhaps it would be better hung in the middle.

He hangs the medal on front of her dress, salutes and steps back. Lulu smiles proudly at the decoration

Lulu 'Tis a great honour, sir. But the first thing I shall do is to pawn Walter's medal ...

Captain Pawn it?

Lulu We're desperate short of money, sir. In fact I am trying to get my old job back, in the pickle onion factory up the street.

Captain (*out front*) Gad! What a waste of womanhood! She deserves something much better than gherkins and wallies! (*He turns to Lulu*) Ma'am, if I may be so bold. (*Turning on the charm*) As an officer and a gentleman of the Twenty-ninth Regiment of Foot, I feel it is my duty—an honour—to look to the welfare of wives of our brave soldiers lost in action. I have a large estate in Worcestershire and have opened part of it as a comfortable home for young war widows. (*He strokes his moustache*)

Lulu Oh! I've never been to Worcester-sheer-shire! How many young widows do you have there?

Captain You shall be the first—I've only just started! It could be a solution to your unhappy plight, I can offer you good food, your own room and a small allowance each month. Will you come, ma'am?

Lulu Good food? Pocket money? And a warm bed to snuggle up to Little Willie?

The Captain's eyes pop!

You bet I'll come!

Captain (*out front*) Gad! She's taken the bait! (*He rubs his hands in anticipation*)

Lulu But wait! What's to happen to my poor old father? He's riddled with lumbago, who will take care of him?

Captain How old is he?

Lulu He's nearly sixty, sir.

Captain Then he's old enough to look after himself! Well, I'll send the old chap a few shillings from time to time!

Lulu Oh, thank you, sir! You are kindness itself!

Captain Well, grab a cloak, let's be off!

Lulu fusses herself tidy and the Captain rubs his hands together eagerly

> *But the door bursts open and in staggers Sam. He is very drunk, his hat is askew, his collar is flapping and his coat is off his shoulders and is buttoned on the wrong buttons. He sways his way down front and barges the Captain off to the right*

The Captain stares in disbelief at the drunken figure who has burst upon the scene

Sam 'Lo Loolie! (*He waves feebly*)
Lulu Don't you call me "Loolie", you drunken old fool!

Sam staggers and sways back to Lulu

Where is the shopping? Where is the bread, the cheese, the milk?
Sam Ah! (*Big explanation*) Wus goin' pass the *Slaughterer's Arms* when that sixpence you gave me, jumped from my pocket and bounced right over the doorstep of the public bar—(*hic*)—it rolled across the floor and through a teeny-weeny crack right under the counter an' finished up by the landlord's feet! Simple!
Lulu Did he give you the sixpence back?
Sam No, he didn't—he picked it up and put it in his cash box—and poured out four pints of old and filthy—(*beer pump action*)—so what could I do? I had to stand there like a fool and drink it!

Lulu aims a blow at her father but he sways away and she misses. Sam staggers over towards the right and collides with the Captain. Sam turns and through the alcoholic haze sees a military figure before him. He stiffly comes to attention and salutes

Good Lord! It's General Kitchener! One eight five four seven three Private Wormpit, reporting, suh!
Lulu That's not General Kitchener!
Captain (*taking charge*) Stand at—ease!

Sam does

Who is this brewer's scarecrow?
Lulu That is my father, sir! Father, this kind gentleman has offered me a place in a young war widow's home in Worcester-sheer-shire—there's food, shelter and pocket money!
Sam What about Little Willie?
Lulu Ooh! He will be well looked after!

The Captain's eyebrows go up

Captain I've got to get rid of the old fool! Private Wormpit!
Sam Suh! (*He clicks his heels, winces*)
Captain Private, you are under my orders. Take this Queen's shilling and return to the—er——(*He snaps his fingers*)

Sam (*side of mouth*) *Slaughterer's Arms*!
Captain Return to the *Slaughterer's Arms* and remain on duty until you are relieved at midnight!
Sam I shall wanna be relieved before then! (*He holds his stomach*)
Captain That is an order!
Sam Yes suh! Very good, suh! (*He salutes and staggers away round the table towards the door*)
Lulu Father! Come back here!

Sam stops by the door

Sam Loolie! Orders is orders! I have accepted the Queen's shilling! If I don't do as the General says I shall be in the glasshouse!
Lulu It'll make a change from the workhouse!

The door bursts open once more. This time in comes Mr Arkwright, the owner of the pickle factory. Dressed in a very loud check suit, complete with spats and a small bowler/derby hat. He is a large, florid man and has a broad North Country accent

His entrance has knocked Sam back round the table and he collides with the Captain; they both finish across to R as Arkwright walks down front to Lulu

Arkwright Hello, young Lulu! Your pa says you want to see me?
Lulu Oh, hello, Mr Arkwright! I *did* want to see you—but I have made other arrangements now.
Arkwright Arrangements? What arrangements?
Lulu You see, my husband was in the army and is lost missing in Africa. I've become a young war widow, and needed money, I did think of asking you for my old job back in the pickle onion factory!
Arkwright A war widow? You? A job in the pickle—? Nay, lass!

He puts a protective arm around Lulu's shoulders, she snuggles in tight

I can think of something much more suitable than the pickle factory—shush!—I know you were the best gherkin-bottler I ever had—but that's not for you now, my dear! Oh, no! Not now!
Lulu Such a lot has happened to me since I left the pickle factory, Mr Arkwright!

Arkwright So it seems—and you must have been good at it too—I see you've won a medal! And you seem to have matured somewhat—if I might say so! (*He cuddles her*)

Lulu smiles at this compliment

No, lass. The pickle factory's not for you! D'you know where I live?

Lulu Oh, yes. The big house, Arkwright Hall.

Arkwright How would you like to live there—instead of 'ere?

Lulu It sounds very grand ...

Arkwright Ooh, ay! Very grand—and very lonely. You see, Lulu, my wife—Mrs Arkwright—is a sort of—er—like a semi-invalid, like. Not a very active woman, you might say. Me? I'm very active! But we both need companionship, you see ...

Lulu Both of you?

Arkwright Ay! Her during the daytime and me during the—— You'll love it at Arkwright 'All! You can have your own bedroom, plenty of good food—why you could even learn to play the piano!

Lulu (*clasping her hands and smiling*) Good food, my own room and me and Little Willie on the piano stool!

Arkwright nearly chokes

Arkwright (*out front*) By jingo! It's on! After all these years! (*To Lulu*) Come on, lass! Get your coat, my horse and cart is outside, waiting!

As Arkwright releases Lulu from his arm, Sam sways over and taps him on the shoulder. Arkwright is surprised to see Sam

Oh, it's you! Sozzling Sam!

Sam Did I Arkwright, 'ear right? I mean, did I 'ear right, Arkwright? Are you offering my daughter food and shelter for companionship?

Arkwright (*thumbs behind his lapels*) An act of charity, old man! An act of charity!

Sam I could do wi' a spot o' charity, meself! (*He holds out a shaking hand*)

Arkwright Here you are, old 'un! (*He pulls a coin from his pocket*) Here's half a sovereign—go and buy yourself a pub!

Sam (*looking at the coin*) Strewth! 'Ere, Arkwright! Did you know *he* has offered Lulu the same—food and shelter and a bit of companionship!

Arkwright Who has?

Sam 'Im over there! (*Pointing*) General Kitchener! Suh!

Sam salutes as the Captain steps across to C *to meet Arkwright coming from* L. *They face each other* C

Captain Captain Harvey Kneetrembler, Twenty-ninth Regiment of Foot!

He salutes and holds as Arkwright offers a handshake

Arkwright I'm Arkwright, the Pickled Onion King!

The Captain alters to a handshake as Arkwright alters to a salute, they change alternatively but never clasp hands and give it up

Now, look here! You keep your military maulers off young Lulu, I've had my eye on her from the first day she started in the gherkin shed! So I've got first claim!

Captain (*wearily*) Put a cork in it, Arkwright! You are dealing with an officer and a gentleman, not a pickle onion salesman! I was here first and the girl is coming with me——

Sam (*on the other side of Arkwright*) To Worcester-sheer-shire!

Arkwright (*to Sam*) Shut up! (*To the Captain*) She's coming to Arkright 'All!

Sam That's right, do right, Arkwright!

Arkwright (*to Sam*) Belt up!

The Captain is enjoying the verbal duel between Sam and Arkwright

Captain Say it again, Sam! (*He smiles, strokes his moustache*)

Arkwright and the Captain grasp each other's jackets and begin wrestling and gasping "She's coming with me". Lulu pushes in between them and stops them

Lulu Please! No fighting over me!

Captain I consider that you are well worth fighting for, ma'am!

Arkwright Huh! One right-hander and I'd knock all those brass buttons off his uniform—and stuff those medals up his——

Lulu Please! There is an easy way to decide.

Captain ⎫
Arkwright ⎬ (*together*) How?

Lulu I'll put it up to Little Willie!

Both Arkwright and the Captain stand pop-eyed. Lulu moves upstage and collects the baby from the cradle and rejoins her two suitors

(*Holding the baby up*) Now, little Willie, which one shall we go with, eh?

Captain } (*together*) {*That* is Little Willie? (*They stare at each*
Arkwright *other*)

Captain A chee-ild?

Arkwright A ruddy nipper?

Lulu Yes, he was born soon after I left the pickle factory!

Captain Never trust a gherkin!

Arkwright Huh! You're in a right pickle now, aren't you?

Sam And you two are a right pair o' wallies!

Lulu hands Little Willie to Sam who holds it out at arm's length rather distastefully and returns it to the cradle. The Captain and Arkwright press Lulu with arguments

As they do so, the door opens and a smartly dressed young man enters

Sam is the only one to spot him

Hey! Look who is here!

The others turn

Lulu Why! It's my Walter!

She runs to him and they embrace warmly

Captain (*to the front*) Lance-Corporal Littlehampton! That's torn it!

Arkwright Her husband? (*Out front*) Just my ruddy luck!

Lulu and Walter walk down front L

Lulu Oh, Walter! Let me look at you! How smart you are in that suit—but where is your soldier's uniform?

Walter The war is over, Lulu! The troops are home again and I have a discharge!

Lulu (*concerned*) Oh, you poor boy! Was it the "Fuzzy—Wuzzies"?

Captain (*nastily*) You are posted as missing, Lance-Corporal, are you sure you are not a deserter?

Walter A deserter? Me? You're a fine one to talk! He sent us out on a suicide mission, and when the natives attacked us he ran all the way back to headquarters!

They all jeer at the Captain

Captain (*blustering*) Well—I—er—had to get another map! (*He backs off*)

Lulu Were you captured, Walter? Or wounded?

Walter No, I was one of the lucky ones. I escaped and as I was creeping away, I fell down this deep dark hole.

He makes a spiralling motion with his finger; they follow his actions, fascinated

It was dark and when daylight came I was down what seemed to be a deep pit—almost like a mineshaft! There was a short tunnel that came to a dead-end and no way up the sides of the pit. I just lay there and thought "This is the end".

Sam And was it?

Lulu hits him

Walter I lay there for several days and nights, growing weaker and weaker, my cries for help growing fainter and fainter! Then after about a week I noticed some little lights shining—twinkling away in the reflected light from above! So I went round and collected all those little lights—(*he picks imaginary objects with his finger and thumb and places them in his other hand*)—and then put them in my pocket! (*He smiles, his eyes vacant*)

Sam He's as daft as a daffodil!

Captain Round the twist!

Arkwright Up the ruddy pole!

Lulu thinks so too!

Walter And then—(*he brightens*)—one morning a local farmer heard my cries for help, he threw a rope down the hole and pulled me up! He took me to a town called Kimberley——

Mutters of "Never heard of it!"

—I showed them my "little lights"—and—well—here I am, home again, safe and sound!

Lulu Never mind, love! I'll take care of you!

Walter No! *I* shall take care of you, sweetheart! Hold your hands out!

She cups her hands and Walter pours the contents of a leather bag into them

Lulu Ah, bless him! He brought home some little lights, just for me!

Walter Little lights? They are diamonds, Lulu—and they are worth a million pounds! And there are more where they came from!

Lulu Diamonds! (*She looks closely at her cupped hands*)

Captain ⎫ (*together*) ⎰DIAMONDS??
Arkwright ⎭

Arkwright Where did you say this place is?

Captain Kimberley—in Africa!

Arkwright Come on! I've got my horse and cart outside! Which way is Kimberley?

Sam, Walter and Lulu each point in different directions and shout "It's that way!" Arkwright and the Captain fight to get out of the door first; Arkwright comes back down to Sam

Do me favour, old 'un! (*He hands Sam a huge bunch of keys*) Look after the pickle factory while I'm gone!

He rushes back out of the door after the Captain

Lulu Who would have thought that my Walter would return home a millionaire!

Walter takes a huge stone from Lulu's hand and hands it to Sam, who is still studying the bunch of keys

Walter Here you are, Pop! This one is for you ...

Sam's eyes pop

Go and buy yourself a brewery!

Sam I think I might do that, I've got a bit of a thirst! (*He rattles the keys*) But I'll have to lock up pickle factory first!

He sways and staggers out of the door

Walter and Lulu are alone. She pours the diamonds back into the leather bag and Walter pops them into a pocket

Lulu And I have a surprise for you!

She goes to the cradle and lifts out the baby and brings him down to Walter. He beams

Here he is, our own little son, William!

She hands the baby to Walter, who after holding it for a few seconds screws up his face with distaste and hurriedly passes the baby back to Lulu and wipes his hands on his suit

He's quite a little man, isn't he?

Walter Nature is a wonderful thing. Just think, all the time I have been away our Little Willie has been growing bigger and bigger!

Walter smiles but Lulu looks at Walter and mouths a silent "Oooh!"

D'you know, all the way home. I kept saying to myself—"I know what I shall have first when I get indoors!"

Lulu rushes upstage and lobs the baby into the cradle and during the rest of Walter's dialogue she removes her outer garments with passion, throwing them behind her with abandon

We couldn't get any in Africa!

Lulu throws off her shawl

And there were none on the boat!

Off comes Lulu's apron

And all the way up on the train, my mouth was watering at the thought!

Lulu nods her head in agreement and hurls her shoes over her shoulders and throws off her cap

And when I came round the corner of the street, I thought to myself—"It won't be long now!"

Lulu mouths a silent "No!" and ruffles her hair over her shoulders, undoes the top button of her dress and slips the dress off her right shoulder. She puckers her lips and snuggles into Walter's left side and melts. He is still happily smiling out front

So when you are ready—(*he claps his hands together and rubs them in anticipation*)—I'll have a nice plate of Arkwright's Onions!

He smiles broadly and nods. Lulu pulls her dress back on her shoulder, stamps her feet in anger and sobs

CURTAIN

First Curtain Call:

Lulu in the centre holding the baby: Walter and old Sam on either side of her: the Captain and Arkwright are on each end of the line. They take the well-deserved applause and the curtains close only to swish open again after a few seconds to catch the cast completely unawares

Second Curtain Call (unexpected):

Lulu is still in the centre but is being flattered and fondled by both the Captain and Arkwright who seem determined to pursue her after the play has ended. Lulu is enjoying every moment of "extra time". Walter has had the baby dumped in his hands and is still holding it at arm's length, turning his head away in disgust and grimacing at the audience. Sam at the other end of the line seems to have thoroughly enjoyed his "boozer's" role for he is busy drinking from a large beer bottle/tankard

After a few seconds the cast become aware that the curtains have reopened and hastily turn to the front and smile, somewhat embarrassed, at the audience. Sam tries vainly to hide the bottle/tankard, Walter holds the baby at arm's length in his right hand, left hand by his side. The Captain and Arkwright reluctantly release Lulu and all three look front and smile

Third Curtain Call (totally unexpected):

The curtains swish open again. Sam is peering into an upturned empty bottle/tankard. The Captain and Arkwright are wrestling in the centre while an impatient Lulu waits to see who is to be her lover. Walter has dumped the baby on the floor and is busy devouring a large plate of pickled onions

FINAL CURTAIN

FURNITURE AND PROPERTY LIST

On stage: Fireplace
Cradle
Rickety table. *On it:* milk jug, jam jar with flowers, telegram
2 old chairs

Off stage: Newspaper **(Sam)**

Personal: **Lulu:** baby, coin
Captain: photograph, medal in box, coin
Arkwright: coin, bunch of keys
Walter: bag of diamonds
2nd curtain call:
Sam: bottle of beer
3rd curtain call:
Walter: plate of pickled onions

LIGHTING PLOT

Property fittings required: *nil*

Interior. A cottage living-room. The same scene throughout

To open: General interior lighting
No cues

THE GREEN EYE OF THE LITTLE YELLOW DOG

(Based upon the poem by Milton Hayes)

CHARACTERS

The Colonel, backbone of the British Army
Ranji, his Indian servant
Major Harrington, retiring adjutant
Belle, the Colonel's beautiful daughter
Captain Quincey Hogg, the new adjutant
Rudyard Singh, rebel leader
Narrator

The action of the play takes place in the Colonel's living quarters in the British fort just north of Katmandu

Time—1882

Running time approximately 20 minutes

AUTHOR'S NOTE

There have been many humorous versions of Milton Hayes' classic poem "The Green Eye of the Little Yellow God". I well remember as a schoolboy listening to Billy Bennett's earthy translation—"There's a broken-hearted woman doing splits in Chu Chin Chow"—and listening, and watching Michael Kilgarriff's hilarious two-man adaption. I would like to believe that the original poem was a romantic version of the actual events that took place and that the following dramatized account is much nearer the truth.

THE GREEN EYE OF THE LITTLE
YELLOW DOG*

The action takes place in the living quarters of the Colonel at the British fort just north of Katmandu. Essential furnishings on stage are a small table with decanter and glasses and a low couch placed upstage L. *An archway to the parade ground is to* R *of the stage and another doorway leads to the rest of the bungalow. The stage is in darkness as the* CURTAIN *opens and a solitary spot beams down on the apron. Into this spot steps the Narrator, who recites the first verse of the monologue*

Narrator "The Green Eye Of The Little Yellow Dog."
There's a one-eyed yellow mongrel
To the north of Katmandu
By the British fort
That stands beside the bog
There's a legend in the regiment
Of that night in eighty-two,
And the green eye of the Little Yellow Dog!

The spot fades allowing the Narrator to step back into the wings as the stage is slowly lit. As it brightens Ranji can be seen arranging the glasses on the table

The Colonel enters R

Colonel Ah! There you are, Ranji! Keep your eyes peeled will you, old chap? I'm expecting Major Harrington over for a farewell drink.
Ranji Colonel Sahib, my eyes are peeling at all times! (*He blinks and rolls his eyes*)
Colonel Do you know, Ranji. I shall miss old Harrington! He's been out here twenty-one years with the old regiment—almost

---

*N.B. Paragraph 3 on page ii of this Acting Edition regarding photocopying and video-recording should be carefully read.

as long as myself! Always did his job in a first-class fashion—
gone downhill these last few years, though. I suppose it's the
strain of keeping these tribesmen wallahs under control. And
the climate——

Ranji If the Colonel Sahib is not minding me saying so, Major
Harrington has countless problems. Biggest problem of all is—
—(*He mimes raising a glass and drinking with a very shaky hand*)

Colonel Ah, yes! He does like a drop of the old Bovril! I hope he
doesn't drink too much tonight at his farewell ball!

Ranji gives an exaggerated lean to the right with his hand to his ear

Ranji Colonel Sahib! I think he comes now! (*He crosses* R)

*Harrington strides on, thrusting Ranji to one side, and salutes the
Colonel*

As he does, Ranji raises a fist behind him in mock aggression

Harrington Good-morning, sir! You wanted to see me?

Colonel 'Morning, Harrington! So this is the big day, eh? This
time tomorrow you will be heading for England, home and
beauty! Twenty-one years! A fine record, Harrington. The
Indian Army owes you a debt of gratitude for your unswerving
loyalty and devotion to duty during these troubled times. You
and me together have kept the flag flying over this outpost of
the British Empire! Tonight, at your farewell ball, I shall have
the pleasure of presenting you with the Regimental Medal of
Honour! (*He beams*)

Harrington (*wiping his mouth*) I would much rather have a drink,
sir!

Colonel Of course! Of course! Ranji!

*But Ranji is all ready for action and is pouring drinks as the Colonel
speaks. He offers the tray*

(*Taking a drink and sipping*) Cheers! The first today!

*Harrington takes a drink, counts off on his fingers, reaches five and
swallows the drink in one draught. He holds out his glass which Ranji
refills*

Harrington The Regimental Medal of Honour, eh? After twenty-
one years of slog, sweat and flies! (*He brushes away imaginary
flies from his head*) I had hoped to take something more valuable

than a medal back with me to England, sir. Something to feast my eyes upon for the rest of my days! Something to grasp with two hands and call my own!

The Colonel looks blank and turns to Ranji. They discuss some matter as:

The Colonel's daughter, Belle, enters from L. *She wears a long gown and a broad-brimmed hat. She smiles at her father*

Ranji salaams. Harrington takes her across DR *out of hearing of the others*

And how is the beautiful Memsahib, this morning?

Belle Very well, thank you, Major!

He grasps her wrist as she turns away

Harrington Belle! Belle, darling! Won't you change your mind? Come with me to England tomorrow—marry me, Belle, and make me the happiest man in the whole world!

She pulls free of his grip

Belle I have already told you, Major. I have no wish to marry you, I have a young man, an officer, in England. When we are ready I shall marry him!

Harrington You will never leave this God-forsaken hole of a country. Your father will see to that! And no right-minded young officer will volunteer for duty out here! Come with me, Belle! I promise you'll not regret it!

Belle I'm sorry Major, but I am already promised to another. But thank you for asking. (*She turns towards her father and Ranji*)

Harrington finishes his drink and gives it to Ranji, who jumps back as Harrington snarls at him

Harrington I must leave you now, sir. I have some packing to do.

Colonel Of course, old chap! We shall see you in the mess tonight!

They salute. As Harrington leaves Ranji takes a distant kick at him

Harrington exits

(*To Belle*) I shall miss old Harrington, m'dear. He's been a jolly good adjutant, twenty-one years out here——

Belle He's a thoroughly unpleasant man! He drinks like a fish——

Ranji does his drinking mime again

—he leers at every white woman——

Ranji mimes the shape of the female body

—and he treats the local natives with utter contempt!

Ranji raises his fist at the departed Harrington

I for one shall be glad to see the back of him!

Colonel I thought you liked the chap. Wondered if he'd ever pop the question to you, m'dear!

Belle He has! Time and time again. But I could never marry a man like that!

The Colonel puts an arm round her shoulders

Colonel There are not many eligible young men in this region, m'dear. And that young officer chap of yours is thousands of miles away in England.

Belle Perhaps one day—when we return home—I shall meet him again . . .

The Colonel shakes his head sadly

Colonel I am destined to finish my days out here, Belle. If you go to England, you must make the journey alone. But I would much rather you stay with your old father.

She kisses his cheek and slowly walks off

The Colonel finishes his drink as the Lights dim to a Black-out

Ranji exits during the Black-out

The spot DR *comes up and the Narrator steps forward and delivers the second verse*

Narrator   The Colonel's daughter, Belle
          A pure, sweet, unspoiled gel
          Her beauty roused men's passion
          Drove them wild
          She spurned the Major as her lover
          Because she love another
          A Lieutenant she had met when just a child.

*The spot dims and the Narrator steps back as the scene is lit once
more. The Colonel is standing upstage*

   Ranji comes on

Ranji Colonel Sahib! There is bright new officer gentleman just
arriving outside! He is very young and very pink!

Colonel Aha! That'll be the replacement for Harrington! A chap
called—er—Hogg! That's it! Captain Hogg! You had best bring
him in, Ranji!

*Ranji scuttles off and returns leading on a tall, pale-looking young
officer. He salutes the Colonel and stands stiffly to attention*

Hogg Good-morning, sir! Captain Hogg, reporting, sir!

Colonel (*saluting casually*) Good-morning, young fella me lad!
Stand easy, stand easy! So you have volunteered for service out
here to become our new adjutant?

Hogg Yes sir!

Colonel Do you realize young man, you could spend the rest of
your military career in this outpost of the British Empire?

Hogg I understood that when I volunteered, sir!

Colonel Well, I'll try and explain the situation out here, young
man. Ranji! (*He snaps his fingers*)

Ranji pours two drinks

   You will take a drink, of course?

Hogg I do not imbibe, sir!

*Ranji looks up and smiles; he swiftly swallows one of the drinks and
hands the other to the Colonel*

Colonel You don't drink? But everybody takes a drink out here!
(*He sips his drink*)

Hogg I only drink lime juice, sir!

The Colonel sprays his drink

Colonel Lime juice? Why we give that to the other ranks—keeps
'em away from the—keeps 'em cool and calm!

Hogg I prefer to be cool and calm, sir!

Colonel Suit yourself! (*He takes another sip of his drink*) This
region up here, Randipore, is inhabited by rebellious tribesmen.
We had a sort of war with their late ruler, the Maharaja, years

ago and a lot of bitterness still lingers under the surface. We are in fact, sitting on a powder-keg, young man! One false move and we could have another mutiny on our hands, so listen carefully! You may have noticed when you entered the fort, a sort of memorial by the gates?

Hogg (*puzzled*) Yes, sir! It looked like a dog, a horrible yellow creature, standing like this . . .

He half-lifts his left leg, the Colonel half-lifts his left leg

Colonel That's it! That's the one! Well, that mongrel dog was the pet of the Maharaja. It was known by the natives as the Gonga Pooch—that's local dialect for sacred dog—but it lost an eye in an accident. Instead of an ordinary glass eye, the Maharaja, being an Indian Prince, had the eye replaced with a large green emerald of immense value. When the old mongrel died they erected that monument to it, right bang outside the fort——

They both half-lift their left legs

—complete with the emerald in the dog's eye!

Hogg That is incredible, sir! With all those native ruffians lurking about outside, d'you mean that nobody has ever tried to steal the emerald?

Ranji salaams and shakes his head

Colonel The local chaps wouldn'd dream of it! Apart from being a sacred animal, the Gonga Pooch has a curse! Anybody taking the stone would die a thousand deaths!

Ranji draws a finger across his throat

You will also notice that the natives always salute the statue——

Ranji salaams

—but ignore the British flag——

Ranji puts his tongue out

—and to keep the peace and appease the natives, we also salute the statue when entering and leaving the fort.

Hogg I find that unbelievable sir! Surely that is against the Queen's Regulations, sir?

Colonel Regulations mean very little when you are surrounded by ten thousand warring tribesmen! So if we don't——

They both salute, half-raising their left legs

—those native wallahs will climb all over this outpost of the Empire and hack us to pieces!

Hogg puts a hand to his throat as Ranji, smiling, draws a finger across his throat

Hogg But, surely, sir! The Maharaja wouldn't dare? He would have the whole of the Army of India after him!

Colonel The Maharaja died some years ago, his nephew now rules the tribesmen, an unsavoury character called Rudyard Singh! And he is waiting for such an opportunity to attack us!

Hogg feels his throat

You will assume your duties tomorrow, young man. Tonight you are invited to the Regimental Ball in honour of Major Harrington, then I'll introduce you to the rest of the chaps. Ranji will take care of your baggage and take you to your quarters. I shall see you this evening!

The Colonel exits R, *followed by Ranji*

Hogg salutes. Left alone, he repeats the half-raised left leg and saluting routine, and feels his throat again. He turns to go off R

As he does so, Belle enters L *carrying her hat. She pauses on seeing the lone figure*

Belle I beg your pardon, I thought my father, the Colonel, was still here.

Hogg begins to turn to the front slowly

Hogg No, miss. But can I help you? (*He faces her*) Captain Quincey Hogg, at your service!

He salutes and smiles at her. She puts her hands to her face in complete surprise

Belle Quincey! You here? What a wonderful, wonderful surprise!
Hogg Belle, my darling!

They embrace warmly. She takes a step back and looks at him

Belle I've prayed every night that somehow, some way, we would meet again—and here you are!

Hogg Belle! You are as enchanting as ever! I once told you I would journey to the ends of the earth to be with you, I have kept my word! Here I am!

Belle But how? Why? It is unbelievable!

Hogg Ever since we met those years ago I have studied the Army lists to see where your father was stationed, always here in Randipore. When I heard that his regiment needed a new adjutant on a long service engagement, I volunteered! The quickest and surest way to be by your side!

Belle But Quincey, your career in England? Your staff job in Whitehall?

Hogg I chucked it all up to volunteer for this posting, so that we could be together. That is—if you will still have me?

Belle Oh, Quincey! You sacrificed your commission in the Post Office Fusiliers just to be with me?

They embrace again and kiss just as:

Harrington enters R

Harrington Well, well, well! (*He crosses behind them to* L)

Hogg and Belle break. Belle is now in the centre

He hasn't been in the fort ten minutes and he is crawling all over the Colonel's daughter! Or is she crawling all over him?

He leers at Hogg who takes a step back

Ranji returns and hovers UR *following the conversation*

Hogg I say!

Belle How dare you, Major! May I introduce your successor as adjutant, and *my* sweetheart—Captain Quincey Hogg, late of the Post Office Fusiliers!

Harrington (*scoffing*) Quincey Hogg? Ha! The natives will love that name! (*He laughs loudly*)

Ranji grins. Harrington walks across R *in front of the other two, then circles round Hogg, looking him up and down*

The Post Office Fusiliers, eh? One of our crack regiments! Seen lots of action, have we? (*He leers over Hogg's shoulder*) What were you in, the Dog Licence Brigade? (*To Belle*) Have you noticed his little pink face and his little pink knees? He'll look good up to his waist in elephant gunge!

Hogg pulls a wry face, Harrington moves L again

Then there's this hell-hole of a country! The monsoons! The unbearable heat!

Hogg fans himself

The rich odours that perculate from the native quarter!

Hogg screws his face up in disgust

And the cursed flies! (*Harrington brushes away imaginary flies*) I've always had bother with the flies!

Belle eyes him and nods agreement

(*To Hogg*) You'll have trouble with flies too!

Hogg half turns away and checks his trousers

And he'll love the food! Unspeakable trash! Vindaloo! Chapattis! Curried goat!

Hogg winces

Huh! The only decent food is what Belle serves at dinner parties—I can't keep my hands off her poppadums!

Hogg (*incensed*) You bounder! It seems to me Major, that you have been drinking! And one too many, if I may say so!

Harrington Of course I've been drinking! Nothing else for a chap to do out here. After twenty-one years on the permanent list you find you are permanently per-per-pie-eyed! (*He puts his arm round Belle's waist*) Come on, Belle! Don't play hard to get with me! Leave with me tomorrow for England!

Hogg (*to Belle*) I say! I've just travelled half-way round the world to be at your side, don't say you are dashing off to Leicester Square first thing in the morning?

Belle Of course not, Quincey! (*She pulls away from Harrington*) Major, for the very last time, the answer is "NO"! I wish to spend my days with Captain Hogg, out here in India!

Harrington You'll regret it, my girl! So will you, Hogg! Understand this, I intended to take home with me what I considered

the "Jewel of the East", you, Belle! But if you will not join me I
shall take home another jewel and God help all those I leave
behind!

Belle How dare you, Major! Ranji! Show the Major to the door!

Harrington Ranji? He's nothing but a jumped-up Punkah Wallah!
Out of my way! (*He makes for the exit* R, *pushing Ranji aside. He
turns before leaving*) At least allow me the honour of one dance
tonight . . .

Belle turns away

Harrington leaves

Ranji aims a kick after he has gone

Hogg What a thoroughly unpleasant fellow! What did he mean,
calling you the "Jewel of the East"?

Belle (*patting her hair*) Just a figure of speech, Quincey! I will
explain to you later! But put Major Harrington out of your
mind, darling. It is you I love and have always loved since that
day we met in Richmond Park!

They embrace and Ranji looks on with keen interest

Quincey! I have longed for the day when you would make love
to me!

Hogg tries to pull away and glances off to R

Hogg I ought really to unbuckle my equipment!

*Belle puts her hand to her mouth and flutters her eyes at his
suggestion. Ranji is most interested*

Belle I want this evening to be an occasion we shall remember for
the rest of our lives!

Hogg You mean——

His face lights up. Belle nods slowly, her eyes closed

Hogg You mean—we shall——?

Belle nods with more emphasis. Ranji rubs his hands

We shall dance the Military Two-Step together? (*He does a
couple of light steps and salutes*)

Belle That wasn't quite what I had in mind, Quincey! (*She* *embraces him again*) This is India, Quincey. A land of hot summer nights where passions run free as a mountain stream! I hope you haven't travelled half-way round the world just to dance a Military Two-Step with me? Tonight we shall drink champagne—(*she mimes drinking*)—and then—the warm tropic night will set the mood!

Hogg is taken aback

Hogg I say! (*He eyes Belle as the penny drops*) I only ever drink lime juice!

She mouths "lime juice" out front, wrinkling her nose. She steps back from Hogg and claps her hands

Belle Ranji!

She snaps her fingers. Ranji springs to duty and pours a drink which he hands to her. She passes it to Hogg

Try this, Quincey! It's guaranteed to work!

Hogg sniffs, then sips the drink. He then swallows the contents of the glass, totters sideways and back

Hogg Belle, there is something I really ought to do!

Belle smiles expectantly

I *must* go and unbuckle my equipment!

With that he salutes, turns right smartly and marches off, tossing the glass over his shoulder

The glass is caught expertly by Ranji in the slips. Belle is furious and stamps her foot

Belle I must be slipping!

Ranji (*trying to be helpful*) Memsahib! You should have tempted him with your poppadums!

Belle turns and snorts with anger. She snatches off her right shoe which she aims at Ranji, who ducks

She turns and rams her wide-brimmed hat firmly on her head, then with chin up she resolutely limps off L

Ranji shrugs and spreads his arms as he speaks out front

What strange ways British people have when making love!

He shakes his head sadly as the Lights dim to a Black-out. Ranji exits during the Black-out

The spot comes up DR *and the Narrator steps into the beam and continues. The sound of an orchestra playing a waltz can be heard in the background*

Narrator   When the ball was at its height
                    On that still and tropic night
                    The Major, encouraged by the hooch
                    Crept outside the fort alone
                    And prised the large green stone
                    From the figure of the little yellow pooch.

The spot fades and the Narrator steps back as the Lights come up

The Colonel enters R, *rather unsteadily. He hesitates by the table, pours himself a drink and continues to* L. *The sounds of the orchestra can still be heard*

Ranji creeps on stealthily and looks around. He spots the Colonel

Ranji Psst!

The Colonel still lurches on

PSST!!

Colonel (*turning back*) Who is? Oh! It's you, Ranji, old chap! Wassamatter?

They meet C, *the Colonel's eyes blinking, Ranji looking right then left before speaking*

Ranji Colonel Sahib! A great calamity befalls us!

Colonel Don't tell me the bar has run dry!

Ranji Infinitely more perilous! There is great commotion outside of fort!

Colonel (*indicating the orchestra*) There's a helluva racket inside as well! (*He sips his drink*)

Ranji Colonel Sahib! There is great sharpening of knives by the natives! Them outside! (*He points off* R)

Colonel Who do you mean? The regimental barber?

Ranji Listen most careful, Colonel Sahib! Some rascally scoundrel has stolen the Green Eye of the Little Yellow Dog!

Ranji claws his left hand to his left eye, withdraws the hand leaving the eye closed tight. The Colonel peers at the closed eye for a second or two

Colonel Stolen? D'you mean somebody's pinched the paw-paw from the pooch?

The Colonel sprays Ranji, who wipes his face

Ranji (*close to the Colonel*) Precisely!

The Colonel gets sprayed and wipes his face

Colonel Good heavens, Ranji! It could mean another mutiny!

Ranji That is what I have been trying to get into your thick British bonce! (*He leans to the right and listens. He clutches his throat*) I think they are coming, Colonel Sahib! (*He glances* R) It is the leader of the mutinous dogs, himself! Rudyard Singh!

Singh enters

Ranji clutches his throat in terror. The Colonel remains cool and British

Colonel 'Evening, Rudyard Singh! Is there something——?

Singh Don't give me that colonial clap-trap, Colonel! Doubtless you have been informed by this miserable son of a pariah——

He spits at Ranji's feet. Ranji jumps back

—that our sacred idol, the Gonga Pooch, has been stripped of its all-seeing eye, the Randipore Emerald! The legend of the Yellow Dog prophesies that blood will flow if the jewel is stolen by an unbeliever! The Yellow Dog has now but one eye Colonel, what shall you do?

Colonel (*casually*) Call it Nelson I suppose!

Singh roars and pulls a knife, Ranji cowers

Singh One word from me and the mob will invade the fort!

Colonel But we are holding a Regimental Ball, old chap!

Singh That is nothing to what I shall hold, Colonel!

He flicks the knife, the Colonel and Ranji step back

Belle comes on from R

Belle What on earth is happening out there? Oh! It's you, Rudyard Singh! (*Coldly*) How nice!

Singh Greetings, beautiful Memsahib! (*He salutes with the knife before his face*)
Colonel Just a bit of a hoo-haa with the native wallahs, m'dear!

Singh grasps Belle's left hand behind her and pulls her before him tightly

Singh Now, Colonel! Perhaps we can discuss terms! You and your force will search and find the missing jewel, or ... (*He brings the knife up before Belle's face*)
Ranji (*shaking his head*) Ooh! Very messy!
Colonel Are you holding my gel as a hostage?
Singh See that the emerald is returned and I shall not harm the beautiful Memsahib! (*He smiles sweetly at Belle*)

Hogg bounces on

Hogg I say! Where is everybody? Just going to do the jolly old Military Two-Step and where are you? Eh? (*He spots Belle being held by Singh*) I say, old thing! You're not having this dance with that native chap are you?
Singh Who is this toy soldier?
Colonel Our new adjutant, chap called Smogg——
Hogg Hogg, sir!
Colonel Yes, Hogg! Just arrived from England!
Singh You have chosen an unfortunate time to arrive, Adjutant Hogg!
Belle Quincey! Some fool has stolen the jewel from the Yellow Dog, I am being held hostage until it is returned!
Hogg The jewel stolen? How very odd! I have just been informed that Major Harrington left the fort fifteen minutes ago on horseback, riding like billy-ho!
Singh The infidel!
Belle The idiot!
Colonel The scoundrel!
Hogg The bounder!
Ranji (*smiling*) Oh, what a clever dickie! (*He nods his head*)
Colonel If that jewel is not recovered, Hogg, we shall have a mutiny on our hands!
Singh You speak the truth, Colonel!
Hogg Then there is no time to lose! *I* shall ride after Harrington

and recover the jewel! Ranji! Saddle a horse, I shall leave at once!

Ranji scuttles off

Belle Oh, Quincey! (*She beams at Hogg*)

Hogg And you, release the Memsahib! I shall bring back your precious jewel, I give you my word as an Officer and Gentleman!

Singh (*spitting on the floor*) That means nothing to me!

Hogg Very well! Scouts' honour! (*He gives a scout salute*)

Singh I accept your word! (*He releases Belle*) You have until daybreak to return the jewel, or . . . (*He passes the knife across his throat*) But remember the legend of the Yellow Dog! All who handle the jewel will suffer the curse of the Gonga Pooch!

Hogg (*flicking his fingers*) I do not believe in your eastern mumbo-jumbo! (*He looks away, uninterested*)

Belle Quincey! (*She embraces him*) Take great care, darling! And hurry back to me! I shall reward you as only a woman can! (*She kisses her fingers and presses them to his lips*)

Ranji dashes on from R, *pointing*

Ranji Captain Hogg, Sahib! Outside waiting is most powerful horse, complete with saddle and giddy-up!

He hands Hogg a small whip which he tucks under his left arm. He salutes

Hogg Time to go, sir! I shall return by daybreak, have no fear!

Singh I shall take you through the gate, or my followers will hack you to pieces!

They exit R, *followed by Ranji*

Belle blows a farewell kiss, the Colonel salutes casually, and sips from his glass

Belle (*her hands clasped*) Father! Did you ever see such braverey? Such devotion to duty?

The Colonel takes another sip

Colonel I think he's a stark staring loony!

Black-out. The spot come up DR. *The Narrator moves into the beam and recites*

Narrator   He returned before the dawn
              With his shirt and tunic torn
              A gash across his forehead, dripping red
              He was patched up right away
              And slept right though the day
              As the Colonel's daughter watched beside his bed.

Then Narrator steps back as the spot dies and the scene is lit Belle is pacing, wringing her hands. The Colonel is studying an empty decanter

  Ranji rushes in

Ranji Colonel Sahib! Memsahib! He is back! Captain Hogg is returned!

He goes off R and returns with Hogg hanging round his shoulder. His shirt and tunic are torn and his body is covered with cuts, his forehead gashed and bloody. He is in a sorry state but still manages a weak salute

Belle   Quincey! Quincey, darling! Did you recover the jewel?
Hogg   (*nodding slowly*) Caught Harrington—twenty miles out—(*he points off*)—his horse shied—threw him—hit his head on a rock—poor chap, died at once! (*He almost collapses*) Found the jolly old jewel—was putting it back in the yellow mongrel—(*he coughs*)—those damn natives attacked me—tried to tell them . . .

He collapses and is supported by Ranji and Belle to the low couch where he is made comfortable

Belle   Brandy! That will help! Brandy!

The Colonel holds up the empty decanter, waves it at Ranji who searches his robes and produces a half bottle of brandy. The Colonel fills a glass and goes to drink it but Ranji points to Hogg. The poor Captain is given the brandy and they watch him dying, then Belle clasps her head and sobs on her father's shoulders

  Ranji walks slowly off shaking his head

  Black-out, during which Belle and the Colonel exit, and a marble cross is set DL

Two spots come up, one DR for the Narrator and one DL illuminating a small cross with "Captain Hogg" inscribed across the arms

Narrator   There'a a one-eyed yellow mongrel
                      To the north of Katmandu
                      And a marble cross inscribed
                      To "Captain Hogg"
                      And a broken-hearted woman

*Belle enters, covered with a black veil. As the Narrator speaks, she
kneels beside the cross and lays a posy of flowers against the plinth*

                      Tends the grave, because she knew
                      'Twas the vengeance of the Little Yellow Dog!

Black-out

                              CURTAIN

FURNITURE AND PROPERTY LIST

On stage: Small table. *On it:* tray, glass decanter of drink, 4 glasses ·
Low couch
Other items such as chairs, plants, drapes, etc. as desired

Off stage: Hat **(Belle)**
Small whip (giddy-up) **(Ranji)**
Marble cross **(Stage Management)**—set during Black-out on
page 34
Black veil, posy of flowers **(Belle)**

Personal: **Singh:** knife
Ranji: half-bottle of brandy

LIGHTING PLOT

Property fittings required: *nil*

Interior. Colonel's living quarters. The same scene throughout

To open: Spot DR for Narrator

Cue 1	**Narrator:** "... Little Yellow Dog!" *Fade spot; bring up general interior lighting—day*	(Page 19)
Cue 2	**Belle** slowly walks off L *Fade to black-out; bring up spot DR*	(Page 22)
Cue 3	**Narrator:** "... when just a child." *Fade spot; bring up general interior lighting—day*	(Page 22)
Cue 4	**Ranji:** "... when making love!" *Fade to black-out; bring up spot DR*	(Page 30)
Cue 5	**Narrator:** "... little yellow pooch." *Fade spot; bring up general interior lighting—evening*	(Page 30)
Cue 6	**Colonel:** "... stark staring loony!" *Black-out; bring up spot DR*	(Page 33)

Cue 7	**Narrator:** "... beside his bed."	(Page 34)
	Fade spot; bring up general interior lighting—early morning	
Cue 8	**Ranji** walks slowly off shaking his head	(Page 34)
	Black-out; bring up spot DR and spot DL on cross	
Cue 9	**Narrator:** "... little yellow dog!"	(Page 35)
	Black-out	

EFFECTS PLOT

| *Cue 1* | **Narrator** begins to speak | (Page 30) |
| | *Waltz music—gradually fade as scene proceeds* | |

COSTUME PLOT

The **Colonel, Major Harrington** and **Captain Hogg:** tropical kit. Bush shirts and khaki shorts will suffice for uniforms. A Sam Browne belt will add period rig for officer. Peaked hats should be worn, or sola helmets, except the Colonel who could be bare-headed. Socks and boots.

Ranji: long, once-white robe tied round waist, with soiled turban. Grubby appearance, tooth missing, unshaven face, perhaps a stringy beard. Bare-footed or sandals.

Belle: tall, elegant young lady in long, flowing gown with broad-brimmed hat.

Rudyard Singh: dark robe as he represents evil, richly embroidered with jewels, held by a wide decorated belt with a knife. Jewelled turban.

Narrator: evening dress or better still, tails.

THE BRAVE BUGLER

or

UP THE KHYBER PASS

A Military Manoeuvre

CHARACTERS

Colonel, the Fort Commander
Captain Cramphorn, his adjutant
Sergeant-Major Bullock, backbone of the army
Daphne, the colonel's daughter
Bugler, action man
Officer, lucky late-comer

The action of the play takes place in a British Army fort on the north-west frontier of India

Time—the 1890s

PRODUCTION NOTES

The play develops into a vehicle for a short, chubby, knockabout comedian to play the Bugler. He must be a good tumbler, hurling himself on from the side of the stage when he repulses the native attack. Somersaults, if possible, but cartwheels and head-over-heels bring him back on stage each time. He must also be able to accomplish a quick change, from his tropical kit into the tattered shirt and shorts. He does not have to play the bugle, as he only manages a few squeaks and honks when he tries. He needs to be short as Daphne needs to be tall; when they are together his head must be at, or below, her shoulder height. Daphne, as well as being tall, is the type of girl that no British colonel in his right mind would allow in a fort on the north-west frontier. Apart from having two hundred British soldiers following her about she is possibly the reason why the tribesmen are trying to break in! Sergeant-Major Bullock is the typical British NCO. He carries out each movement with parade-ground precision and speaks with the drill sergeant's bark. His stomping, barking approach terrifies the officers. The Officer who comes on at the end and steals Daphne from the Bugler can be played by the Chairman (if used during a Music Hall programme) or by a well-known local personality. I know a doctor who enjoys a small walk-on part with a company each year, his appearance is always greeted with prolonged applause. In return he is willing to loan his stethoscope for medical sketches!

THE BRAVE BUGLER*
or
UP THE KHYBER PASS

The scene is a British Army fort on the north-west frontier of India in the 1890s

There is a backcloth depicting fortress walls and the hills beyond the battlements. UL is a veranda with a door leading into the "Officer's Mess". Upstage is a small bamboo table and two bamboo chairs

At the time of the action the local hill tribes are waging a constant harrassment of the occupiers of the fort and occasionally gunfire is exchanged, but today all is quiet. Despite what amounts to be a siege by the tribesmen, the occupants, being British, carry on a normal existence, determined that the beastly tribesmen shall not alter their long-established routine

The door from the "Officer's Mess" opens and the Colonel strolls out into the sun-baked square followed by his adjutant, Captain Cramphorn. They walk down front, yawn and stretch, look around the fortress walls, tap their legs with their canes, sigh and depict utter, utter boredom. After a few moments the Colonel speaks

Colonel Another beastly warm day, Cramphorn. What's on today's orders? Hm? Nothing too strenuous I trust?

Captain (*scanning through his notebook*) Let me see, sir. Ah, yes! According to regimental orders we ought to have an early morning parade followed by a platoon commanders' meeting at eleven hundred hours. (*He replaces the book*)

Colonel Not another parade, Cramphorn! Dash it all, we had a parade only last week. (*He taps his leg with his cane*)

Captain But, sir, we are supposed to have a parade *every* day while on active duty——

---

*N.B. Paragraph 3 on page ii of this Acting Edition regarding photocopying and video-recording should be carefully read.

Colonel I know, I know, Cramphorn! But it is such a tiresome
affair. I walk up and down the ranks, I look at all the faces of the
chaps and they look back at me—(*he walks across and back
again*)—they must feel the same way about it as I do.

Captain I haven't heard anyone complaining, sir.

Colonel Of course not, Cramphorn, they are a jolly good bunch of
chaps, that's why! They come out here togged up with all those
belts and—and buckles and things—(*He indicates with his free
hand*)

Captain Equipment, sir!

Colonel Yes, and that too! All polished and shiny, then I look at
them and they look at me. Then they go away and take the belts
and—things off and—it must be as boring for them as it is for
me! Let us do something different today, Cramphorn! (*He tucks
his cane under an arm and claps his hands together and rubs them*)
What shall we do? Hm?

Captain I beg pardon, sir, but there is still the platoon commanders' meeting——

Colonel That's another boring affair. I never know what to say to
the chaps—I mean I've said it a hundred times already——

Captain One hundred and fourteen times, to be exact, sir.

Colonel All about being British, showing the flag, the outposts of
the Empire, play up, play up and play the game! I mean, I've
said it so many times . . .

Captain (*with a worshipping smile*) But you say it *so* well, sir!

Colonel (*smiling and nodding*) Yes! I *am* pretty good, aren't I?

They both nod and smile. The Colonel claps his hands again

Well then, Cramphorn, what shall we do today?

Captain (*echoing to himself*) What shall we do today? (*He snaps
his fingers and looks around for inspiration*)

Colonel I know! We'll have a polo match—a few chukkas will
buck us up no end! (*He beams*)

Captain We can't, sir. Sorry, but we lost the ball, remember?

Colonel (*dismayed*) So we did. Won't those native chappies give it
back? (*He gestures to the right*)

Captain I'm afraid not, sir. They said if we want our ball back we
shall have to fetch it ourselves!

Colonel Jolly bad show that, no sporting instincts!

Captain Definitely not cricket!

Colonel That's it! A game of cricket! The very thing! Get the bat and ball and stumps out——

Captain (*restraining the Colonel*) We can't play cricket either, sir. We lost that ball as well—remember?

Colonel Oh, yes. So we did. The natives won't return it?

Captain No, sir. You do hit the ball pretty hard, sir! (*He nods approvingly at the Colonel*)

Colonel (*nodding and smiling*) Yes! I *am* pretty good, aren't I?

They both nod and smile

Captain (*idea at last*) I've got it! (*He snaps his fingers*) How about a jolly old game of cards?

Colonel Cards? *Cards*? Not very exciting, Cramphorn, a game of *cards*? I never play cards.

Captain Something simple, sir. How about a game of—snap?

Colonel Snap? *Snap*? (*Uninterested*) Never heard of it!

Captain It's jolly exciting, sir. I'll teach you!

Colonel Oh, very well. What is it called? Snap?

They walk upstage to the table and sit down

Jolly good thing you are here, Cramphorn. Thinking up these wheezes to amuse a chap.

Captain (*smiling*) Yes—I *am* pretty good aren't I?

They nod and smile

Colonel Without these diversions a chap could go . . . (*He waves a hand above his head*)

Captain Doolally, sir?

Colonel Do whatie?

Captain Doolally, sir. A local term, it means—(*his index finger describes a circle at the side of his head*)—means going bonkers!

Colonel Oh! You mean potty!

Captain Exactly, sir. And a quiet game of snap will relieve the boredom.

They sit and twiddle their fingers, tapping on the table top

Colonel Shall we need cards for this exciting game, Cramphorn?

Captain Why of course, sir! How forgetful of me!

He rises and walks down front, calling off L

Sergeant-Major! Sergeant-Major Bullock!!

He resumes his seat with a reassuring smile while the Colonel is utterly bored

> *Heavy footsteps are heard and from the left comes Sergeant-Major Bullock. He stomps very loudly and with exaggerated military precision marches across the stage to* R, *where he executes a series of right turns until he is beside the officers. He comes noisily to a halt and salutes and stamps his feet*

Sergeant-Major Sergeant-Major reporting, *sah!*

The officers cringe and flinch at every step and cower away when he speaks

Captain Good—good-morning, Sergeant-Major. Do you think you could find the Colonel and I a pack of playing cards?

Sergeant-Major *Sah!* (*He takes two steps sideways to the right and searches his pockets and brings out a pack of cards. He takes two steps to the left, stamps his feet, and holding the cards erect in his left hand he salutes again with his right*) One pack of cards, playing, officers, for the use of, *sah!*

They cower again and Cramphorn takes the cards

Colonel Sergeant-Major . . .
Sergeant-Major *Sah!*

They flinch

Colonel Sergeant-Major, I know it's none of my business, but— and you probably derive a great deal of pleasure from it—but— do you think you could conduct yourself in a more restrained fashion? I mean, all this stomping and shouting can give a chap a bad head—I mean—do you *have* to do it?

Sergeant-Major It is according to the Military Training Manual, *sah!* I been doing it nah for twenty-free years, *sah!*

He stomps and salutes, they cringe

Captain He is a lovely mover, sir.
Sergeant-Major Yus—I'm pretty good, ain't I?

All three nod and smile

Captain Absolutely splendid!

Colonel First-class—but could you do it just a little quieter? What with the stifling heat—it could send a chap—er—what's that word, Cramphorn?

Captain Doolally, sir.

Colonel Yes, could send a chap—doolally, you know.

Sergeant-Major I hunderstands, *sah*. Has you wish, *sah*! (*He stamps his feet and salutes and makes his way* L *with a series of turns just as exaggerated and as noisily as before. As he reaches* L *to exit he raises his left arm and points off*) That man there! Walk properly! Head up! Chin in!

He exits still shouting

Colonel Thank goodness he's gone! (*He shakes his head*)

Captain Yes, sir. He could give one the screaming ab-dabs!

Colonel The screaming what?

Captain The screaming ab-dabs, sir.

Colonel What are the "screaming ab-dabs"?

Captain It's another local term, sir. It means ... (*He again describes a circle with his forefinger to his head*)

Both Doolally!

Colonel You seem to be picking up the local dialect easily, Cramphorn, it must be jolly useful having two languages.

Captain I find it very helpful when conversing with the local tribesmen, sir. Shall we play cards?

They face each other across the table. Cramphorn shuffles the cards and explains the game

We have half each, sir. We lay the cards face up alternately, if we lay a card and its number matches the card on the table, you call out "Snap!" and you win the cards, and so on. (*He splits the pack in two and lays them down*)

Colonel You have more cards than me, Cramphorn!

Captain Sorry, sir! (*He hands over one card*) Now I'll lay first!

They lay their cards and after only a few Cramphorn yells "Snap" and picks up the cards. This goes on until Cramphorn has all the cards and the Colonel has none

That's it, sir!

Colonel That's *it*? I haven't any cards!

Captain (*with a huge smile*) I know, sir. I've won!

Colonel You've won? But I never had a look in!

Captain Haha! You've got to be jolly smart to beat me at snap, I can tell you!

Colonel Indeed! (*He rises to his feet sternly*)

Cramphorn stands beside him, his smile vanishes

I don't want to pull rank on you, Cramphorn, but I am your Commanding Officer.

Captain I realize that, sir. It wasn't my intention to win every time, I must have got carried away. But I *am* pretty good, aren't I?

Colonel (*gruffly*) Yes.

Captain Would you care for another hand, sir? Now you have the hang of the game you will probably win.

They sit and resume playing. After a few cards have been laid Cramphorn prompts the Colonel

S-S-S-Sn-Sn——

Colonel Snap! Got you that time, Cramphorn!

Captain Well done, sir!

They continue playing, each winning in turn

The Colonel's daughter, Daphne, drifts on from the door of the Officers' Mess. She is a tall, well-endowed girl wearing a diaphanous long gown with rather a daring neck line. She floats across the stage and turns, reaches the upstage side of the bamboo table. She leans forward over the card players

Daphne Good-morning, Daddy!

Both officers turn and look at her

Both SNAP!

She kisses her father's forehead

Daphne What a lovely, lovely day! (*She stretches her arms upwards*)

Colonel Daphne, my dear. I wish you would not wander round the barracks dressed like that.

Daphne Why not, Daddy?

Colonel My dear, there are close on two hundred soldiers in the fort and you are the only white gel for miles around. You could easily turn the men's heads—you could start an uprising!

Captain (*fingering his collar*) Easily!

Daphne (*running her hands over her hips*) Yes! I *am* pretty good, aren't I?

Colonel Now don't you start! Stay indoors and don't stand too close to the men!

Daphne Why not, Daddy?

Colonel Why not? 'Cos you'll give them the—what's that phrase, Cramphorn?

Captain The screaming ab-dabs, sir.

Colonel That's it! They will get the screaming—things—and it's not good for them!

Daphne I have no need to stand close to *them, they* stand close to *me*!

She smiles and stretches again. The Colonel buries his head in his hands and Cramphorn turns away, loosening his collar and fanning his face

(*Looking down at the cards*) Snap!

The officers turn quickly and study the cards. They take them and begin another game as Daphne watches

As they play Sergeant-Major Bullock enters from L. *He sways his way on the same circuitous route as before but stamps his feet rather weakly. He halts by the table and gives a weak stamp and a half salute. He has a long native spear buried in the small of his back*

Colonel That was much better, Sergeant-Major!

Captain Yes, nicely done!

Daphne (*pointing to the Sergeant-Major*) What is that funny thing, Daddy, sticking out of him?

They drop the cards and rise quickly

Captain Where?

They inspect the Sergeant-Major up and down

Daphne In his back!

They walk round behind the Sergeant-Major and turn him sideways so that the spear can be seen from front

Captain I say, sir! He has a spear in his back!
Colonel By jove, I believe he has! (*He fingers the shaft of the spear*)
Is it painful, Sergeant-Major?
Sergeant-Major (*with a brave face*) Only when I stamps me feet
and salutes, sah!

He stamps his feet and winces with pain, they support him

Colonel Where did it come from, Sergeant-Major?
Sergeant-Major One of them natives frew it at me, *sah*!
Captain I say, jolly good shot wasn't it? (*He smiles*)
Colonel Rather, those natives *are* pretty good, aren't they?
Sergeant-Major Them natives, *sah*! They are revolting! (*He sways*)
Colonel I agree with you—by jove! Do you mean they are—
Cramphorn! This could be it! An attack! Call the Bugler!

Both officers stand aimlessly as the Sergeant-Major sways across to
DL *and croaks an order*

Sergeant-Major Bugler! At the double!

The Bugler, a short figure wearing a pith helmet and carrying a
bugle, trots on and stands down C. *He shuffles to attention*

Daphne runs over L *of the Bugler and places an arm across his*
shoulder

Daphne Oh, Daddy! What a lovely little trumpeter!

The Bugler goes cross-eyed. The Colonel and Cramphorn come
down front

Colonel Daphne! Put him down!
Daphne (*pouting*) But, Daddy! I've always wanted my own little
soldier—specially one that plays something!
Captain I can play snap! (*He smiles at Daphne*)
Colonel Be quiet, Cramphorn. Sergeant-Major, tell the Bugler to
sound the alarm and battle order!
Sergeant-Major Bugler—you 'eard!

The Bugler raises the bugle to his lips and inhales. As he starts the
bugle call Daphne places a hand on his cheek and tickles his ear. No
sound comes from the bugle only a slow release of air. He tries three
times and can only manage a few odd notes

Captain Huh! Not a very good trumpet player, is he!

Colonel Try again, man!

Daphne gives the Bugler a tight hug and he emits a loud squeak from the bugle

Come along man! They are getting closer!

Bugler (*eyeing Daphne, and with a high-pitched voice*) That's why I can't blow my bugle, sir!

Colonel Dammit man! Sound the call to arms!

With Daphne caressing him the Bugler manages a few distorted squeaks and growls from his bugle

Sergeant-Major Sah! The men! They have run into the barracks and locked the doors! They refuse to fight!

Captain There's a tricky one for you, sir!

Colonel By jove! The tribesmen are attacking and we have no troops to fight them!

Daphne (*stroking the Bugler's shoulder*) What about my little trumpeter, Daddy!

Sergeant-Major All volunteers—one pace forward!

Everyone except the Bugler takes a step backwards leaving the Bugler out front

Colonel Well done, young feller! Take this man's name and have him mentioned in dispatches!

The Bugler goes through silent protests as they gather round him

Captain (*removing his revolver and handing it to the Bugler*) Here you are old chap, it might come in handy!

Colonel Yes, you could be up against it out there!

Bugler (*eyeing Daphne*) I'd much rather be up against it in here!

Sergeant-Major (*still swaying*) Come along my lucky lad! For Queen and Country! Up and at 'em!

The Bugler makes a grab for Daphne but is held back by the officers. They point to the right

Colonel That way, through the main gate!

The Bugler turns pleadingly to Daphne. She kisses her fingertips and presses him to his lips

This spurs him on, he winds himself up and with another distorted blast on his bugle he dashes off R

The others watch him leave, Daphne waves and the Sergeant-Major sinks to his knees

What were we doing before this skirmish, Cramphorn?
Captain Er—we were playing cards, sir. Snap! And I was winning!
Colonel Oh, yes? We'll soon see about that!

They return to the card table and continue their game. From now until the end of the action they play cards and the game becomes rather heated, fists thrust under noses and tunics grabbed and threats made in mime. As the battle for the fort increases in tempo so does the card game. During the attack, the Sergeant-Major crawls on his knees to the right and encourages our hero, while Daphne produces a comb and combs her hair while the battle for the fort rages

Our bugle-blowing hero has in fact gone to meet an army of ferocious hill tribesmen and soon returns on stage by way of a somersault (a head-over-heels from the wings to the centre will be effective). His shirt and shorts are cut to ribbons and he looks a sorry sight, but Daphne blows him a kiss and he winds himself up again and charges off R, *blowing rude noises from his bugle. Screams, shouts and gunfire are coming from off* R *and our hero staggers back on, his left arm in a sling and huge bandage on his head, both are bloodstained. Daphne takes a medal from her father's tunic and comes down and pins it on our hero. He screams as the pin enters his chest. She blows another kiss and he flies off again, then suddenly all is quiet. No more screams or gunfire. Our hero returns in triumph. Daphne clasps her hands and beckons him to the Officers' Mess. As they reach the veranda the door to the mess opens and half a dozen spears are thrust out of them—those dastardly tribesmen have gone round to the other side of the stage!*

Sergeant-Major Bullock also returns from R *with another spear in his back and crawls across to the left shouting encouragement to the Bugler who engages the enemy spears through the open doorway. He beats them off and Daphne applauds his bravery, coming round and standing between him and the open doorway. A long brown arm reaches out and grabs her and drags her to the door where several brown arms reach out and brown hands caress her body. She stands with her back to the door, her eyes rolling in rapturous delight. Our hero, the Bugler, drags her away and thrusts at the hidden tribesmen with a spear and they withdraw. He steps back and the hand reappears beckoning Daphne to the doorway. She steps to the doorway with her back to the audience and hands embrace her waist and shoulders and she appears to be enjoying the attentive tribesmen. Our hero is enraged and winding himself up again he pulls her aside and fights off the spears, vanishing through the doorway. Several screams are heard and our hero returns and throws a heap of captured spears in front of the Officers' Mess as he struts to c and blows a loud unintelligible victory blast on his bugle. Daphne looks disappointed and stands hands on hips*

The card game has progressed from heated arguments to violent aggression; the Colonel has the Captain across the card table and is slowly throttling him as cards drop from the Captain's limp hands. Sergeant-Major Bullock has by now expired UL, the two spears too much for even his stout constitution and he slowly sinks down saluting as he goes

A distant bugle is heard from off R and Daphne smiles across and with arms outstretched moves towards the Bugler. He, expecting his reward, reaches out and puckers his lips only for Daphne to pass by and advance further to R

  As she does, a magnificently-dressed Officer in scarlet tunic with sword and medals enters R

The Officer meets Daphne and they embrace warmly. The newcomer faces the front and winks at the audience

Officer Trust me to get the best part!

He embraces Daphne once more. She snuggles into him as the poor Bugler is searching, arms out front for his rewarding kiss. Upstage, the Colonel has finally disposed of the Captain who lies limply across the bamboo table, the Colonel throwing odd playing cards at the prostrate body

CURTAIN

Curtain Calls:

The cast take the applause in the established manner, but they are quite unprepared for the second curtain call. This catches the cast unawares and the Colonel and the Captain are at each other's throats. Sergeant-Major Bullock is on his knees saluting, wild-eyed and near to exhaustion. The little Bugler and the newly-arrived Officer are disputing the affections of Daphne, shaking each other whilst Daphne is trying to separate them. They then realize the curtain has opened once more and turn rather sheepishly to the audience and smile and take another bow

CURTAIN

FURNITURE AND PROPERTY LIST

Scenery: Backcloth depicting interior of fort, showing parapet and battlements, and the hills beyond
Small flat painted to represent the exterior of the "Officers' Mess" with a door opening inwards and a veranda on the front

On stage: Small bamboo table
2 bamboo chairs

Off stage: Spear in back **(Sergeant-Major)**
Bloodstained sling and head bandage **(Bugler)**
Attacking tribesmen's spears **(Stage Management)**
Another spear in back **(Sergeant-Major)**
Captured spears **(Bugler)**

Personal: **Colonel:** cane, medals
Captain: cane, revolver, notebook
Bugler: bugle
Daphne: comb
Officer: sword, medals

LIGHTING PLOT

Property fittings required: *nil*

Exterior. A fort. The same scene throughout

To open: Bright, general sunlight

No cues

EFFECTS PLOT

Cue 1   **Bugler** dashes off R; **Colonel** and **Captain** resume card
game   (Page 50)
Sounds of attacking force—gunfire, screams etc.

Cue 2   **Daphne** pins medal on **Bugler**; **Bugler** exits   (Page 50)
Cut attack noise

Cue 3   **Bugler** engages enemy spears L   (Page 50)
Attack noise off L

Cue 4   **Bugler** pulls **Daphne** aside and fights off spears,
vanishing off L   (Page 50)
Cut attack noise

Cue 5   **Sergeant-Major** expires UL   (Page 51)
Bugle call off R

COSTUME PLOT

Colonel and **Captain:** tropical kit, khaki shirts and shorts, socks
and boots. Both wear peaked hats and Sam Browne belts. The
Captain has a holster for his revolver.

Sergeant-Major: khaki shirt and shorts, socks and heavy boots.
Leather belt or webbing belt blancoed. Peaked hat with peak very
low over eyes.

Daphne: long flowing diaphanous gown with low-cut neckline.
Long hair which she combs constantly during the battle.

Bugler: khaki shirt and shorts—these should be extra-long in the
leg so that they almost cover his knees. Socks and boots, if possible
puttees. A sola or pith helmet, a size too big.

Officer: the most magnificent uniform the company can muster,
complete with busby, gold braid and medals.

NELLIE'S NIGHTLIGHTS

A Victorian/Edwardian Comedy

CHARACTERS

Bessie Larkin, long-suffering housewife
Nellie Larkin, her sweet, unspoilt daughter
Corporal Clem Larkin, late of the County Yeomanry
Mr Henry Goitre, unscrupulous moneylender
Mr Wallace Coughtree, benevolent employer
Mrs Sopwith, Coughtree's housekeeper
Mr Russell Spurgeon, Victorian "Whizz-Kid"

The action of the play takes place in the Larkin's living-room and the entrance hall of Coughtree Court

Period—1902

Running time approximately 42 minutes

ACT I*

The scene is the Larkins' living-room in their humble dwelling on Tramway Terrace. Midday

It is a dingy room with a fireplace UC, *a door leading to the kitchen* UR *and another door leading to the street* UL. *A tall table holding a potted plant (aspidistra) is by the kitchen door, an old kitchen table and two chairs are* C

Mrs Bessie Larkin is tidying the room. She stops sweeping as the sounds of a marching band can be heard, it grows louder and the strains of "The Soldiers of the Queen" and cheering crowds pass by the house and fade in the distance. She stands the broom against a wall and dabs her eyes with a small handkerchief

The street door opens and her young daughter, Nellie, rushes in. She points excitedly to the street

Nellie Mother! Mother! Did you hear them? Did you see them?

Mrs Larkin smiles and nods

I followed them all the way from the station to the Town Hall! The band was playing, the crowds were cheering, the flags were waving! The County Yeomanry are home at last, Mother!

They hug each other

Bessie Did you see your father?
Nellie I couldn't be sure—they look so alike in uniform. But it was a wonderful sight!
Bessie He will be home very soon, go and make us all a nice hot drink. Your father will want something warming when he arrives!
Nellie I know! I shall make us mugs of hot cocoa—Father will enjoy that.

---

*N.B. Paragraph 3 on page ii of this Acting Edition regarding photocopying and video-recording should be carefully read.

She exits through the kitchen door

Bessie stays down front, clasps her hands and looking upward mouths a silent prayer for the safe return of her husband

As she smooths her apron the street door bursts open and in lurches Corporal Clem Larkin of the County Yeomanry. He has had a few drinks but is not too drunk—yet! He is in uniform and has his right arm in a heavily padded sling. He greets his wife

They embrace and she looks aghast at his injured arm

Larkin Hello, old girl!
Bessie Clem! Oh, my poor Clemmie! What *have* they done to you?
Larkin (*sadly shaking his head*) It was them Boers, Bessie! They done for me! My right arm is shattered! Useless!
Bessie (*hands to her face*) Will it always be——?
Larkin 'Fraid so, old girl. And I've gotta honourable discharge from the County Yeomanry—they've no further use for me in the army. Bessie! I'm done! Finished! Just a shadow of the man you used to know!

As Larkin shakes his head sadly, Bessie turns away from him, wiping a tear from her eyes. While she is turned Larkin whips his "shattered" arm from the sling. His hand holds a spirit flask which he raises to his lips, takes a hurried swig and returns it to the sling. He blinks his eyes, and executes an exaggerated lurching routine. Bessie rushes to him in alarm

Bessie Clem! Clem! Whatever ails you?
Larkin It's just one of my "funny turns" Bessie, something I have learned to live with!

Bessie is in the depths of despair. Her husband home from South Africa with a "shattered" arm and now suffering from "funny turns"! She hugs him

Bessie Oh, Clem! My poor Clem! With you back home again we were hoping to return to an orderly, secure life! (*She pauses*) I—I don't know how to tell you this—but, Nellie and I are in a lot of trouble!

He pushes her away and stares in disbelief

Larkin Trouble? *Both* of you? (*He stares pop-eyed out front*)

Out comes the flask once more, a quick swig and another "funny turn". Bessie watches his lurching with dismay

(*Recovering*) Trouble? What kind of trouble?

Bessie Money troubles, Clem. While you have been away these three years, we've been desperate short of money——

Larkin Short of money? *Short* of *money*?

Bessie nods

Why, I sent you four shillings this past year, four shillings last year and three shillings the year before! What did you do with it? Fritter it away on fancy clothes?

Bessie Young Nellie and I have nought but what we stand up in! We've lived like paupers these past three years. But I'll not blame you, Clem! You've had your own hardships to bear——

Larkin Ay! (*He nods*) Those Johnny Boers gave us a real runaround! I've seen some fighting. Some of my mates was wounded—some was killed. I am one of the lucky ones, I've only got a shattered arm——

Bessie turns away giving Larkin the chance for another quick swig from the flask and a "funny turn"

Three years of living rough and fighting rough! I was there when Ladysmith was relieved——

Bessie (*looking away*) The poor, poor woman!

Larkin —and I saw Baden-Powell march up from Mafeking! They were proud moments, Bessie. Now, I am honourably discharged and for services rendered, the medals I wear on my chest and two sovereigns as a parting gift. I gave my all for my Queen and country—God bless her—and that's all I have to show for it!

Bessie But you are back home now, Clem. Back home with me and Nellie, we are a family once more and we should be thankful for that small mercy!

Larkin Ay!

Bessie But you return to a troubled house, Clem. To be truthful it can hardly be called our own house any longer.

Larkin Not our house? What do you mean, Bessie?

Bessie Like I was saying, we were desperate short of money while you were away. We had to ask Mr Henry Goitre to tide us over——

Larkin Not "Grasping" Goitre the moneylender?

She nods sadly and turns away, Larkin takes a quick swig at the flask, does a "funny turn" and comes back to Bessie

Bessie Mr Goitre loaned us ten pounds against the deeds of the house and we haven't been able to clear the debt. In fact, what with interest and compound interest we owe him three times what we borrowed—and we have already paid the ten pounds . . . (*She sobs into her hands*)

Larkin Henry Goitre! Huh! I remember his old man—the old skinflint! Shylock we used to call him! I'll soon deal with him! (*He forgets his "shattered" arm, pulls it from the sling and adopts a fighting pose*)

Bessie Threats will not move Mr Goitre, Clem! We have until this evening to settle our debt with him. If we fail to find the money—(*she sobs*)—we shall be cast upon the streets!

She breaks down sobbing. Larkin replaces his arm in the sling

We tried, Clem! The Lord knows we tried! I even went back to my old trade——

Larkin Not——?

Bessie (*nodding*) Scrubbing floors! And our Nellie, bless her little heart, she has brought money home——

Larkin (*raising his eyebrows*) She didn't——?

Bessie (*nodding*) She did! She took herself a job!

Larkin Our little Nellie? A working girl? She's but a child! (*He stretches out his left arm level with his chest*)

Bessie Not any longer, Clem. Our little Nellie is a grown-up young woman. You've been away a long, long, time!

Larkin (*looking round*) But where is the girl? Where is my little Nellie?

Bessie I'll fetch her, she's in the kitchen making you a nice mug of hot cocoa!

She walks UR *and puts her head through to the kitchen as if talking to Nellie. Larkin looks out front and mouths the word "cocoa" and screws up his face with disgust. He takes another quick swig and does a "funny turn" before Bessie turns back*

Nellie enters carrying a tray with three steaming mugs of cocoa. She places them on the table and beams at her father

Larkin Nellie! My own sweet little Nellie!

They hug each other and Larkin becomes aware that Nellie has matured during his absence

My word! How you've grown while I've been away!

Nellie does a "twirl" for him

Bessie A real grown-up young lady, Clem!

Nellie (*beaming*) Yes, Father. I'm almost twenty-one!

Larkin How the years slip by! One moment you're a child, the next moment you're a—(*He shakes his head and wipes away a tear*)

Nellie And I go to work! I'm employed by Mr Wallace Coughtree, I'm a wick-trimmer in his candle factory!

Larkin A wick-trimmer in a candle factory? Why, Nellie, that's skilled work! I'm right proud of you, I never thought you capable——

Nellie Oh, Mr Coughtree, my employer, gives me personal tuition every day. He stands with his hands over my shoulders coaching me in my work.

Larkin I always thought of you in a counting house, not Coughtree's Candle Factory.

Nellie Oh, Father! My employer, Mr Coughtree, is such a kind benevolent man. And working with the candle wax keeps my hands so soft and smooth—Mr Coughtree tells me so, several times a day!

Bessie smiles warmly at her daughter, but Larkin feels it is time for another swig and "funny turn"

Mother! What ails Father?

Bessie (*trying to shield her daughter from Larkin's antics*) 'Tis nothing to fret about, my love! Just one of your father's "funny turns"!

Larkin (*recovering*) But what about our debt, Bessie? I am useless with my shattered arm!

Nellie (*turning away*) Poor Father!

Bessie Mr Goitre has asked for settlement today, Clem. Our agreement terminates at nine p.m. sharp. We have nine hours to raise the money, or we shall be homeless!

She breaks down and sobs. Larkin pulls his left hand from his pocket

Larkin Here are the two sovereigns given me by the Yeomanry—
and—a South African ha-penny!

*Nellie turns her back to the audience and lifting the hem of her dress,
rummages. She turns round smiling*

Nellie And here's a whole shilling! I've been walking to and from
work each day!

Bessie You sweet child!

Larkin (*touched*) You make me feel so—so——! What with my
shattered arm and "funny turns"!

*He turns away dejected. As Bessie comforts him a loud hammering
comes on the door*

Bessie That'll be him! Henry Goitre comes for his money! (*She
opens the door*)

*Henry Goitre strides in. He half raises his hat to Bessie and Nellie,
going over to* R

Goitre (*spotting Larkin*) Well, well, well! So the conquering hero
returns! Huh! I saw you today, Larkin! Strutting through the
town, band playing, flags flying, people cheering! A soul-stirring
sight to be sure! But we all come down to earth with a bang—the
bands have stopped playing, the flags are not waving and the
crowds have stopped cheering! You are back to the realities of
civilian life!

Larkin Give it a rest, Goitre!

Goitre *Mister* Goitre, if you don't mind!

Larkin (*pointing to the stripes on his arm*) *Corporal* Larkin, *if* you
don't mind!

Goitre Huh! You go off to play soldiers in sunny South Africa
leaving your family without two copper coins to rub together.
But for my financial help they would have withered and
perished! But settlement day is here, *Corporal* Larkin! (*He takes
a document from his inside pocket*) The deeds of your humble
dwelling in return for the ten pounds your good lady wife
borrowed from me! (*He offers the document to Larkin*)

Bessie But we have more than repaid the ten pounds, Mr Goitre!

Goitre waves a finger at her

Goitre Interest, dear lady! Interest! You cannot expect to borrow money without paying interest on the loan. And, interest on the interest, and so on and so forth!

Bessie But it is never-ending! We shall never escape your clutches!

Larkin holds out the two sovereigns

Larkin Here yar, *Mister* Goitre! Two golden sovereigns and a South African ha'penny, and—(*he pulls the two medals from his chest and offers them with the coins*)—and the two medals I won in the war!

Goitre (*scoffing*) Huh! Medals? What good are medals for paying the rent? Take 'em down the pawnshop, Larkin! You'll get five shillings for them—if you're lucky! (*He sneers*)

Larkin (*choked*) Five bob? Five bob at the pawnshop? Why, our dear old Queen would turn in her grave if she knew that! D'you mean I've been shifted, shouted, shunted, shipped, shaved, shot, shelled, shattered—sh-sh-sh—(*he splutters on incoherently, finally whipping out his flask, having a quick swig and doing an elaborate "funny turn" close to Goitre*)

Goitre (*retreating in alarm*) Good heavens!

Bessie Take no notice, Mr Goitre, it's just one of my husband's "funny turns"!

Goitre More like a chronic case of "Brewer's Elbow" if you ask me! Come on, Larkin! Pull yourself together man!

Bessie What is our alternative, Mr Goitre?

Goitre Sadly, you will forfeit your house as settlement.

Bessie How much do we owe you?

Goitre (*consulting his notebook*) Let us see. Ten pounds loan at fifty per cent interest per annum, plus accumulative interest and annual increments, carry two, all the rest have thirty-one—is— er . . .

He begins rapid calculations in his book. Larkin and Bessie do simple sums on their fingers while Nellie beams and:

Nellie Twenty-nine pounds, fourteen shillings and three-pence ha'penny!

The other three jump back at her rapid calculation

Bessie Our Nellie was always good at figures!

Goitre (*out front*) Especially her own!

Larkin We don't have the money, Mr Goitre, give us more time!

Goitre The deadline is nine o'clock tonight!

Bessie But what will become of us? Where shall we go?

Goitre Well, I expect our brave soldier boy will find some cosy corner in a four-ale bar and spend the rest of his days recounting his heroic deeds in South Africa! You, Mrs Larkin, can earn your keep in the workhouse scrubbing floors! (*He sneers*) I understand you are an experienced scrubber!

Larkin But what about our Nellie?

Goitre Ah! The lovely Miss Nellie Larkin! (*He crosses and stands behind her talking over her right shoulder*) With her sweet attractive personality and her nimble brain, *I* shall be pleased to find a place for her in my counting house!

Nellie smiles broadly out front

Bessie But where shall she live?

Goitre Oh, I expect my housekeeper will be able to find a small room for her in my house. Then we shall be able to spend our evenings together, going over figures!

He runs his hands across her shoulders and down her arms. She flutters her eyelids and smiles

Nellie Right! That's settled then, shall I pack a bag?

Larkin Hold on! Hold on! I'm not having this! Putting my wife in the workhouse and carting our Nellie off to your house and going over her figure! Ho, no! I'm not a fool you know, Goitre! I'm one of the Shropshire Sharpshooters!

Goitre Shropshire Sharpshooter! Bah! You couldn't hit a haystack from ten feet! You shall be on the streets tonight! I have already made plans to dispose of this property by midday tomorrow!

Bessie Sold over our heads? You heartless creature!

Goitre sneers at them as a loud knocking comes on the street door. Larkin sways his way to the door and opens it

Mr Wallace Coughtree, the proprietor of the Coughtree Candle Company, and Nellie's benevolent employer, enters

Coughtree Good-day, sir!

He raises his hat to Larkin who staggers away. He then goes down front and raises his hat to Bessie and Nellie

Good-day, madam! Ah! Miss Larkin! How do you do? (*He takes her hand*) What lovely soft hands you have, my child——
Nellie Mother! Father! This is my benevolent employer, Mr Wallace Coughtree!

Bessie gives a bobbed curtsy as Larkin comes down front. Coughtree offers his hand to Larkin who takes the "shattered" arm from the sling and is shaken by Coughtree. It is a firm handshake and Larkin is shaken like a rag doll. Goitre moves to R

Coughtree Do pardon this intrusion into your house, Mrs Larkin. But a matter of some importance has arisen at the factory and I need to consult with your daughter—what lovely soft hands she has—er——
Goitre And what brings you to Tramway Terrace, Wallace Coughtree?
Coughtree Hah! I thought you might be here, Goitre, carrying on your filthy trade! This dear, sweet child has told me of your financial plight, Mrs Larkin.
Larkin Our Nellie told *you*?
Coughtree I encourage my employees to come to me with their problems. As well as being an employer I ask my girls to come with me with their worries, I am always ready to help them if I can.
Bessie How very kind you are, sir.
Larkin Are you going to lend us some money, Guv'nor?
Coughtree (*as he eyes Nellie*) That remains to be——
Goitre Watch old Coughtree! He'll have the clothes off your backs!

Bessie covers up with her hands, Larkin grasps his uniform but Nellie smiles, gives a little "Oo" and raises her eyebrows

Larkin What did you want our Nellie for, Guv'nor?
Coughtree Oh, yes! The lovely Miss Larkin—what lovely soft hands—er—the other day whilst I was helping your daughter with her wick-trimming, she made an exciting suggestion to me!
Larkin (*with suspicion*) Did she now?

Nellie nods

Coughtree Indeed she did! We, at the Coughtree Candle Company, have spent years trying to perfect the "long-life" candle. A candle that will burn for hours on end, be cheap to produce and not be of immense size—such as we are making now!

He demonstrates the size by stretching his arms vertically. The others watch with great interest

But your daughter, Mr and Mrs Larkin, has solved the problem!

Bessie ⎫
Larkin ⎭ (*together*) She *has*?

Coughtree Such a clever young lady! Her suggestion has resulted in the development of our latest product. (*He displays a small nightlight on the palm of his hand*) This is it!

Bessie, Larkin and Goitre peer at the small circular wax disc Coughtree holds

Goitre (*scoffing*) So that's it, eh? Huh! (*He folds his arms*)

Coughtree So small, yet so effective! And they will be named after the young lady who suggested them—they shall be called—"Nellie's Nightlights"!

Nellie gives a big "Oh!". Her parents join hands and smile. Goitre gives another "Huh!" and studies his fingernails

Furthermore, each wrapper shall bear a picture of Miss Larkin with the slogan—"The Face That Flickers In A Thousand Bedrooms!"

The Larkins smile

Also—and this gives me great pleasure—I offer this document—(*he produces a folded paper*)—as an agreement to pay Miss Larkin fifty per cent of the profits from "Nellie's Nightlights"!

Bessie and Larkin sneer at Goitre and Coughtree takes the opportunity to kiss Nellie's hand

Goitre Watch him! There's a catch in it somewhere!

Coughtree Stay out of this, Henry Goitre!

Nellie Shall I be rich and famous, Mr Coughtree?

Coughtree Without a doubt! And yours will become a well-known face—in bedrooms! There is however one trifling matter to be decided!

Goitre Here comes the catch, wait for it!

They ignore him

Coughtree We have to decide upon the size and capacity of the nightlight. Our experimental department have been—er ...

Larkin (*brightly*) Experimenting?

Coughtree Er—exactly! But the nightlight must be tried in precise domestic conditions, on a bedside table, in a bedroom during the cool hours of darkness! Then we shall be able to decide upon the size, the type of wick and the make-up of the wax compound.

The Larkins nod in agreement as Coughtree explains the technical problems

So! I invite you Miss Larkin, as my partner in this venture, to join me this evening at my residence, Coughtree Court. There, you and I shall conduct this experiment with "Nellie's Nightlight"!

Nellie Burning on your bedside table?

Coughtree Ye-es!

Nellie Beside your bed?

Coughtree Ye-es!

Nellie With us sitting on the bed during the cool hours of darkness?

Coughtree Ye-es!

Nellie Waiting for the light to go out?

Coughtree Ye-e-es!

Nellie Well! That's settled then! Shall I pack a bag?

Goitre Wait! Wait! (*To Larkin*) You are involving your daughter with this old scoundrel!

Larkin You mind your own business! She is his partner!

Nellie (*to Coughtree*) I'm just a sleeping partner, aren't I?

Coughtree's eyes pop

Coughtree (*out front*) Yes! And make an old man happy!

He touches Nellie's "lovely soft hands", Bessie smiles approvingly. Larkin has a quick swig and does a "funny turn", returning to the front

Goitre "Nellie's Nightlights"! They will never catch on, Coughtree! Do you know why I want this property? I shall tell you! I have a client who wishes to acquire this—apology for a home. He is going to demolish it and build a tram shed!

All A *tram* shed!

Goitre Yes, you may have noticed that the horse-trams turn round out there and the tram lines terminate right outside this house!

He points over the footlights. The others lean forward and peer down int the front rows of the audience and nod agreement

Well, my client, a prosperous and inventive young business man, intends to operate a new tramway system through the town. This is the only site suitable for a tram shed and by this time tomorrow I shall be selling the freehold to him. Nothing can stop the sale!

Bessie Does that mean that trams will be running through our living-room?

Goitre One every ten minutes!

Bessie (*hands on hips*) Huh! I'm not having tram passengers gawping at us having our dinner!

Larkin Hey! That means that people on the upper deck will be able to see us lying in bed!

He and Bessie are indignant, Nellie seems to relish the idea

Coughtree Who is this mystery client of yours, Goitre?

Goitre None other than Mr Russell Spurgeon, the innovator and proprietor of the "All Electric Tramcar Company"!

All "All Electric Tramcars"?

Larkin has a quick swig and a "funny turn"

Goitre Yes, indeed! "All Electric Tramcars"! We are now in the twentieth century, we are stepping out of the Victorian era. Vast strides have been made and people are demanding progress! The Electric Tramcar will provide a cheap, almost silent and very fast service through the town, and this very room will be their tram shed!

They stand stunned. Coughtree recovers

Coughtree How much is the outstanding debt, Goitre?

Goitre again fumbles with his book, Bessie and Larkin try their fingers once more

Nellie Twenty-nine pounds, fourteen shillings and threepence ha'penny!

Bessie She has a quick brain!

Coughtree And lovely soft—er—in recognition of our agreement—(*he waves the document*)—I propose to advance royalties
to the sum of thirty pounds to Miss Nellie Larkin for the use of
her name, and sweet face, for "Nellie's Nightlights"!

*Nellie, Bessie and Larkin applaud. Goitre sneers. Coughtree hands
the money to Nellie, she passes it to Bessie who hands it on to
Larkin, who spits on it for luck and smacks it into Goitre's hand*

Larkin Here yar, *Mister* Goitre!

Goitre You'll live to regret this, Coughtree! I shall spoil your little
plan yet! You shall see! You haven't heard the last of Henry
Goitre!

*He passes the deeds to Larkin, who tries to read the print through
drink-hazed eyes*

Sneering, Goitre leaves through the street door

Bessie hugs Larkin while Coughtree holds Nellie's soft hands

Bessie You saved our roof from being sold over our heards, Mr
Coughtree. However shall we repay you?

Coughtree holds and pats Nellie's hand

Coughtree (*out front*) I expect I shall receive my just reward! But
now I must leave you, I have to prepare for this evening. Until
eight o'clock, Miss Larkin!

*He kisses her hand, raises his hat to Bessie and Larkin and leaves
by the street door*

Bessie What a kind, generous man your employer is, Nellie! We
have settled our debt with Mr Goitre and you have become a
sleeping partner!

Nellie nods

Just what *is* a "sleeping partner", Nellie?

Nellie I'm not too sure—but I expect I shall find out as time
passes!

Bessie We are a happy united family once more, what else can we
want?

Larkin (*groping in his pocket*) I want one of those sovereigns, I
need some more medicine for my "funny turns"!

He sways his way to the street door, flask in his "shattered" hand.
Bessie and Nellie watch him leave as

the CURTAIN *falls*

ACT II

The entrance hall of Coughtree Court, the private residence of Mr Wallace Coughtree. Later the same evening

There is an entrance door R and a large baronial fireplace up C. The first few treads of a flight of stairs which leads to the upper floor can be seen L. A chair stands by a small table on which stands a bottle of champagne and two glasses. There is also what appears to be a very small nightlight on the table

Mrs Sopwith, Coughtree's housekeeper, is busy sweeping the floor

Coughtree, dressed in a long night-shirt under a dressing-gown and topped by a woollen night-cap, comes on from L beside the staircase. He hustles Mrs Sopwith

Coughtree Come on, you old harridan! Get finished and get out! I don't want you hanging about here tonight!

Sopwith I'll bet you don't, Wallace Coughtree! Not with that young lady up there in your bedroom!

Coughtree Keep your voice down!

Sopwith Oh, I ain't afeared o'you! I've known you since you was that high—(*she holds out her hand, waist-high*)—you was scheming then and you are still at it now! You are just like your father, he was a scheming lecherous old man—and nobody knows better than me! If I had any sense I would warn that young lady about you and your——

Coughtree raises a hand as if to strike her

Coughtree Shut your trap! Miss Larkin and I are partners in a business enterprise, and this evening we shall be carrying out—er—a—er—commerical experiment!

Sopwith (*leaning on her broom*) Ho! That's what they calls it now is it? A commercial hexperiment! Huh! That's not what they called it in my day!

Coughtree I never knew you had a day!

Sopwith I did you know! I had my day all right—and many of 'em!

And me nights as well! He! He! He! I suppose she is one of your fancy lady employees as you call 'em? You pay their wages do you? The wages of sin I calls it! The wages of sin!

Coughtree tries to quieten her

Coughtree Take your witch's broom and get out of here! Here take this—(*he pulls a coin from his pocket*)—go and drown yourself at your favourite gin palace!

Sopwith Ooh! (*She looks at the coin*) A half-sovereign is it? You *are* keen to get shot of me! With a half-sovereign to spend I shan't be around for a few days. (*She leers close to his face*) Your secret will be safe with me! (*She rests the broom by the door and turns*) Just remember one thing, Wallace Coughtree, as you climb them stairs. Your old heart is not as strong as it used to be! You could go just like your old man— (*she snaps her fingers*)—he used to burn the candle at both ends, you want to light it in the middle as well! Just like him, you could be ten feet tall one minute and six feet under the next! Mark my words!

Coughtree hustles her through the doorway

Mrs Sopwith exits

Coughtree locks and bolts the door. He walks across L *and looks up the stairs, feels his heartbeat and thumps his chest*

Coughtree Don't stop tonight, you fool! Keep going!

He opens the bottle of champagne and fills the two glasses. A loud "Coo-ee!" comes from up the stairway. He walks across to the foot and holds out a hand

Nellie walks slowly down. She is wearing a long night-gown with a shawl across her shoulders and a small mop-cap on her head

You look exquisite, my dear!

Nellie smiles coyly

Nellie Are you sure we have to wear our night-clothes for the experiment, Mr Coughtree?

Coughtree We have to try and create a true bedside atmosphere, my dear. It is the only way!

Nellie I suppose you are right. (*She giggles*) But you do look funny in that silly little hat!

Coughtree tries to retain his dignity

Coughtree This is my usual night attire, I like to keep warm in bed.

Nellie Me too!

Coughtree Then I am sure we shall! Was the room to your liking?

Nellie I think it is the nicest bedroom I have ever seen! Such a great big bed! Why do you have such a great big bed if you sleep alone?

Coughtree Ah! I—er—I tend to toss and turn in my sleep, I like plenty of room!

Nellie But why two pillows?

Coughtree Er—I—I sometimes sleep one side of the bed and sometimes the other!

Nellie But why do you have "WC" embroidered on your pillows?

Coughtree Because they are my initials—"WC"—Wallace Coughtree!

Nellie Oh, I *see*! But it's a lovely bouncy bed—I tried it! I hope you don't mind!

Coughtree Not at all! Not at all! You must try it again, later!

Nellie And such a lovely marble washstand. We haven't anything like that at home. But one thing did puzzle me, Mr Coughtree, why do you have that big square mirror suspended above your bed? (*She draws a square above her head with her hands*)

Coughtree Ah! That! Yes! Well, I sometimes like to shave in bed, my dear!

Nellie Oh, what a jolly good idea!

Coughtree Now, my dear. I think we should drink a toast to our new enterprise. I have prepared some champagne!

Nellie Ooh! I've never tasted champagne! I always drink warm milk before going up to bed, it makes me sleep so soundly.

Coughtree (*out front*) We are not drinking milk tonight! Here my dear! (*He hands her a glass*) A toast! Here's to "Nellie's Nightlife"—er—I mean "Nightlights"!

He sips his drink, she empties her glass

(*Out front*) Another one like that and she'll have her father's "funny turns"! (*He refills her glass*) Drink it more slowly, my dear. You will find it very stimulating!

Nellie I know! I'm all warm and bubbly inside!

They sip their drinks

Coughtree I think we should make ready for our task upstairs.
(*He takes her hand and begins to walk her to the stairs*)
Nellie I want to thank you again, Mr Coughtree, for your
generosity to my parents, and as for asking me to take part in
this experiment, well——
Coughtree (*patting her hand*) Tush! Tush! My dear, let us just say
that I couldn't do it without you! (*He picks up the nightlight*) I
thought perhaps we should start with this small prototype
nightlight.

Nellie peers at the tiny disc

Nellie It is very *small*, isn't it? That won't last more than an hour,
and we shall be in the dark for almost nine hours! Whatever
shall we do?
Coughtree Oh, I expect we shall think of something.
Nellie I know! We could play a game!

Coughtree nods approvingly

We could play "I Spy"!

His face drops

You know! I spy with my little eye—something beginning
with——
Coughtree Yes! Yes! Miss Larkin! Please! Please! Bring your drink
and let us make our way upstairs!

*He moves to the bottom tread and takes her hand. She takes a final
look round the room*

Nellie (*chanting*) Nighty-night! Sleep tight! See you in the morning! My mother says that to me every night, Mr Coughtree!
Coughtree Come, my dear! Up the stairs! (*He helps her up the first
two stairs*)

Nellie vanishes from sight

*Coughtree glances round the room, thumps his heart to keep it going
and taking a deep breath, he starts to follow Nellie. He has just taken
three steps when there comes a loud hammering on the front door*

(*From the stairs*) Go away! I'm going to bed!

The hammering persists and he reluctantly comes down the stairs and crosses to the door which he unlocks and unbolts

  It flies open and Larkin and Henry Goitre burst in. Larkin, by now the victim of many "funny turns" is well drunk

Larkin Hello, Coughtree, old coughdrop!

He sways down R. *Goitre studies Coughtree's night attire*

Goitre Haha! Coughtree! Caught you in the act, eh?

Coughtree points to the stairs

Coughtree I was just about to——
Goitre I *know* what you were just "about to—"! That is why we are here!
Larkin S'right!
Goitre Put paid to your little scheme, have we?

Nellie comes down the stairs with her drink

Nellie Father! Mr Goitre! Hello! I was just going to play "I Spy" with Mr Coughtree!
Goitre "I Spy"? "*I Spy*"?

Coughtree shrugs resignedly as Larkin has a swig and does a "funny turn"

Coughtree What is the meaning of bursting into my private residence and causing this uproar? Miss Larkin and I were just about to——
Goitre And we stopped you just in time!

Larkin sways over to Goitre and points to Nellie

Larkin Thash my daughter! 'Lo Nellie! She's 'is shleeping partner! All ready for bed!

Nellie waves back and smiles

Coughtree Will you gentlemen please leave! Or shall I send for the police?
Goitre You wouldn't dare!

Coughtree shrugs

  I've come along with Larkin to stop your little game and to tell you your plan has misfired!

Coughtree Little game? Misfired? What do you mean?

Goitre Playing "I Spy" with Miss Larkin, and saving their home from becoming a tram shed! Huh! I have just concluded a deal with Larkin to buy his property for the sum of one hundred pounds!

Larkin 'Sright! (*He nods and sways*)

Coughtree But why? In heaven's name why? They are perfectly happy there, why take away their home? Where shall they live?

Goitre With one hundred pounds they can buy another house and make way for the Electric Tramcar Shed! Progress must not be halted!

Nellie sits on the stairs sipping her drink. Larkin tries to follow the conversation, nodding or shaking his head

Coughtree Progress? Who wants progress? Electric Trams whirring their way through the streets! They will never catch on anyway! Mark my words!

Goitre Oh, no? Electricity is here to stay, Coughtree! Your days as a candle manufacturer are almost over, soon the whole world will be ablaze with light! Electric light!

Coughtree Electric light? (*He puts his hand to his mouth, uncertain*) No! No! It cannot be!

Goitre Incandescent glass bulbs with a filament that will illuminate a room at the flick of a switch! "Let there be light!" (*He flicks an imaginary switch*) And there shall be light! Your empire of wax candles will melt before your very eyes, Coughtree! To be blunt, old man, your business isn't worth a candle! Ha! Ha!

Coughtree clutches his heart, thumping it

Coughtree Electric tramcars! Electric lights? Whatever next?

Larkin (*brightly*) Electric gas stoves?

Nellie comes down the stairs to Coughtree

Nellie Can it be true, Mr Coughtree?

He shakes his head

Will there be no more candles? Are "Nellie's Nightlights" finished?

Goitre Finished before they started! Obsolete! A product of a bygone age! A new generation arises, Coughtree's candles and nightlights are a thing of the past! Museum pieces!

Coughtree staggers and clutches his heart, Nellie supports him

Nellie Are you all right, Mr Coughtree?

Coughtree Just when everything seemed to be going so well, this happens. Here, my child—take the agreement—(*he hands over a paper from his pocket*)—for what it is worth! It will remind you in years to come of what might have been! And don't think too unkindly of an old man's dreams and fantasies! (*He kisses her hand, giving her the document*) What lovely soft hands you have——

Nellie Does it mean that my face will no longer "flicker in a thousand bedrooms"?

Coughtree (*smiling weakly*) You almost "flickered" in mine! Get dressed, young lady, and take your father home!

He sits on the chair, his head bowed, a broken man. Nellie places an arm round his shoulder

Nellie That was very cruel of you to upset Mr Coughtree like that, Henry Goitre! I think you are a horrid little man and I never want to speak to you again! You have spoiled everything!

Goitre That was my intention, Miss Larkin! Don't you understand? Telling us you were going to play "I Spy" in his bedroom! Huh!

Nellie (*stamping her foot*) We could have played all sorts of games! He has a big suspended——(*She begins to draw a large rectangle above her head and describes it*)

Coughtree places a hand on her arm, stopping her. He screws up his eyes and shakes his head. A loud hammering comes on the front door. Goitre opens it

> *In dashes the eccentric figure of Mr Russell Spurgeon. He is dressed in a leather coat with a peaked hat, goggles, gaiters and gloves. He sports a large handle-bar moustache and strides down front grinning broadly. He stands and whirrs both hands round, clock and anti-clockwise in a flat circular movement. He is at the controls of an "All Electric Tramcar"!*

Coughtree (*weakly*) Who the blue blazes is that lunatic?

Goitre Ladies and Gentleman! May I introduce Mr Russell Spurgeon, the innovator and proprietor of the "All Electric Tramcar Company"!

Larkin, in his alcoholic state, sways to the front and grinning broadly imitates Spurgeon, his hands whirring, his body swaying. Spurgeon watches approvingly

Spurgeon Well done, sir! Absolutely splendid! Have you ever driven an "All Electric Tramcar"?

Larkin (*stopping whirring*) Driven one? I've never even seen one!

Spurgeon But you have just demonstrated perfectly the skills and science of controlling a "Mark One All Electric Tramcar"! Quite remarkable! Why, you even sway just like a tram driver!

They sway together

All tram drivers sway like that! You're a natural!

Larkin Am I? I've been swaying like this ever since I first went into a pub!

Spurgeon Tell me, sir. Are you still engaged by the Military?

Larkin No, sir! I gotta 'orrible discharge!

Spurgeon Well, never mind, old chap! I am engaging a team of first-class reliable fellows, with skill, enthusiasm and expertise to drive my "All Electric Tramcars"!

Larkin I'm your man, Guv'nor! Show me your tramcar and point me in the right direction!

Spurgeon Good man! Report on Monday morning!

Larkin Yes, sah! (*He salutes, then pulls out his flask, has a swig and does a "funny turn"*)

Spurgeon And now, Goitre, what news? Have you secured the premises?

Goitre I have the deeds, Mr Spurgeon. The transaction is complete.

Spurgeon Excellent! First class! I have to give you four hundred pounds for the property and your commission of ten per cent.

As they exchange documents, Nellie rises and walks across c

Nellie Excuse me, Mr Spurgeon. Did you say four hundred pounds for the property?

Spurgeon I did, young lady. That was the agreed price with the vendor!

Nellie But the vendor is my poor old father, here, and Mr Goitre has only paid one hundred pounds for the property. Is there some mistake?

Larkin S'right!

Spurgeon Is that true, Goitre? Have you given this poor man just one hundred pounds for his property? I instructed you pay him four hundred pounds, plus your usual commission. What do you have to say for yourself?

Goitre I—I—er—meant to give him the rest—a genuine mistake on my part, Mr Spurgeon, believe me, sir!

Nellie You are a cheat, Henry Goitre! Trying to swindle my poor old father out of three hundred pounds!

Goitre blusters

Spurgeon Shall I call the police, miss? 'Tis a case of fraud and criminal conversion——

Goitre Please, Mr Spurgeon—Miss Larkin! Don't call the police! The shame and the humiliation would be too much to bear! Here, take the rest of the money—(*he passes a purse to Nellie*)—I am deeply ashamed!

Spurgeon Then leave the district, Goitre! I shall spread the word of your dishonesty, you are a ruined man!

Goitre bows his head in shame as Nellie hands the purse to her father

Larkin S'welp me!

He whips out the flask, takes a swig and does a fantastic "funny turn" finishing next to the broken figure of Coughtree, still holding the flask. Coughtree takes the flask, rises and takes a swig. He does a "funny turn" and finishes up beside Larkin. Goitre crosses and takes the flask and drinks

Goitre I'll take the easy way out!

He does a "funny turn" and finishes in line with Larkin and Coughtree. Then all three, just like a trio of dancers, do a sway and "funny turn" routine together. They then stand shoulder to shoulder facing outwards (forming a triangle) and slowly, by supporting each other they slide down to a sitting position. With heads bowed they sit motionless

Nellie Oh! They have all caught father's "funny turns" now!

Spurgeon I'm sorry, miss, that your home is to be demolished to make way for a tram shed. But I'll make it up to you somehow! (*He pauses*) I know what we'll do! Each of my "All Electric

Tramcars" shall carry the name of a beautiful woman painted along its side and your name shall be on the very first tramcar!

Nellie claps her hands with delight

What is your name, miss?

Nellie (*coyly*) Miss Nellie Larkin.

Spurgeon Then the very first tramcar shall be named "Miss Nellie Larkin"! Am I forgiven, miss?

Nellie I am overwhelmed!

Spurgeon Also, when the first "All Electric Tramcar" leaves the shed and the Lord Mayor cuts the yellow ribbon, you, Miss Larkin, shall pull the switch to set the wheels in motion! And— you shall ride on the front of the very first Electric Tramcar to go through the town!

Nellie stands hands to face, mouth open

We shall speed away from Tramway Terrace——

Spurgeon once more demonstrates the skills of a tram driver, both he and Nellie sway together

—down through the narrow High Street, over the cross roads— our bell ringing! Past the recreation ground and the war memorial, under the railway arch and up the Market Place to the Town Hall!

Nellie How exciting, Mr Spurgeon! My, you do cut a dash in your goggles, gaiters and gloves!

Spurgeon puffs out his chest and grins

Shall I wear goggles, gaiters and gloves for the tramcar ride?

Spurgeon Of course you shall, Miss Larkin! Er—and you had best wear a dress too—it is very draughty on the front of a tramcar!

Nellie So many things have happened to me today, you would hardly credit it!

Spurgeon eyes her night attire

Spurgeon May one ask why you are dressed ready for bed, Miss Larkin? Or shouldn't one ask such a delicate question?

Nellie Oh, poor Mr Coughtree and I were about to begin a business partnership. I was to become his sleeping partner.

Spurgeon raises his goggles and peers at Nellie

Spurgeon Ask a silly question—(*He looks round at Coughtree*) Is that the old codger there?

Nellie nods

Is he—?

Nellie I think so. His candle empire has melted!

He takes a long look at Nellie

Spurgeon (*out front*) I'm not surprised!

Nellie We were to form a new company. Here are the papers!

She hands the documents to Spurgeon, who reads them as Nellie drones on

I was going to be rich and famous, but with the coming of electric lights the Candle Company has crashed and "Nellie's Nightlights" will no longer be a commercial proposition——

Spurgeon Miss Larkin, it says here—"That upon the demise of Wallace Coughtree, all his shares and stock in the Coughtree Candle Company are to be transferred to—you"! And all his worldly goods and property he bequeaths to you "for your kind smile and gentle nature, and your lovely soft hands"! The old codger has left you everything, lock stock and candle! This house—the business—the whole Coughtree empire!

Nellie But with the coming of electric light, surely the business is worthless?

Spurgeon Nonsense— It won't happen overnight, people will be using candles for years to come!

Nellie But what about "Nellie's Nightlights"?

Spurgeon They will sell like hot cakes!

Nellie Then my face will still "flicker in a thousand bedrooms"?

Spurgeon takes a long wistful look at Nellie

Spurgeon (*out front*) I'd say it was a racing certainty!

Nellie Then there is no time to lose! We must continue Mr Coughtree's work and experiment!

Spurgeon Work? Experiment?

Nellie *You* shall join me in Mr Coughtree's bedroom, we shall light this nightlight and see how long it will burn——

She drags him across the room to the foot of the stairs

—now don't let me down! I am relying on you for your cooperation and advice! Oh, and bring that bottle of champagne, we shall be up there all night!

She mounts the first stair as Spurgeon stands open-mouthed as her proposal sinks in

Spurgeon D'you mean—me—and you—up there?

Nellie What else could I mean, you silly little man! (*She climbs another stair and turns again*) One thing more, Mr Spurgeon. Bring your shaving brush with you—there is this huge mirror over the bed!

She once more describes the rectangular mirror above her head and vanishes up the stairs

Spurgeon stands going over the events of the past few moments. He points to himself then up the stairs and draws the rectangle above his head and mouths the word "mirror". He points to the champagne and his eyes widen, a broad grin spreads across his face. He goes through his tram-driving routine with enthusiasm and then tosses his leather hat and goggles across the room followed by the gloves and gaiters, then the coat. He takes a step towards the stairs, turns and goes back for the champagne bottle and the two glasses

Nellie (*from upstairs*) Mr Spur-geon!

Spurgeon (*smiling broadly at the audience*) Coming, Miss Larkin!

He trots off upstairs

The three slumped figures of Coughtree, Larkin and Goitre slide slowly to their right, each one falling across another's legs. They lie still as——

the CURTAIN *falls*

FURNITURE AND PROPERTY LIST

ACT I

On stage: Fireplace
Kitchen table
2 kitchen chairs
Tall table. *On it:* plant
Broom (for **Bessie**)

Off stage: Tray with 3 steaming mugs of cocoa **(Nellie)**

Personal: **Bessie:** handkerchief
Larkin: 2 sovereigns, coin, medals, spirit flask, arm sling
Nellie: shilling
Goitre: document, notebook, pencil
Coughtree: nightlight, document, coins

ACT II

On stage: Baronial fireplace
Small table. *On it:* bottle champagne, 2 glasses, nightlight
Chair
Bottom few treads of flight of stairs
Broom (for **Mrs Sopwith**)

Personal: **Coughtree:** coin, document
Goitre: document, purse
Spurgeon: document

LIGHTING PLOT

Property fittings required: *nil*

2 interiors. A living-room and an entrance hall

ACT I Midday

To open: General interior lighting

No cues

ACT II Evening

To open: General interior lighting

No cues

EFFECTS PLOT

ACT I

Cue 1   After Curtain has risen   (Page 57)
          Marching band playing "The Soldiers of the Queen"
          and cheering crowd—becoming louder than gradually
          fading

ACT II

No cues

COSTUME SUGGESTIONS

Bessie: black high-necked dress with long white apron. Her hair would probably be in a "bun".

Nellie: women rarely went out without a hat and Nellie would have worn a large floral or wide-brimmed hat whilst watching the procession, removing it when arriving home. A high-necked white blouse and black skirt in Act I. For Act II, an ankle-length nightgown and small night-cap, a shawl across her shoulders.

Larkin: late of the County Yeomanry, he is still in uniform. A red tunic and blue trouser dress uniform would be excellent — with a pill-box hat. If khaki uniform try for a white helmet and don't forget the puttees. He would sport the ribbons of the Queen's and King's South Africa medals, better still medals themselves. His sling for the "shattered arm" would need to be padded or stiffened along the bottom — when he removes the arm he wants an easy, quick movement. Any fumbling when pulling out or replacing the flask will cause laughs in the wrong place.

Goitre: the business man of the day would wear a top hat. Goitre, not quite in the upper bracket, will wear a snappy curly brimmed bowler hat. A cut-away, high-lapelled jacket and sport a watch-chain across his waistcoat.

Coughtree: still clinging to his Victorian way of life will wear a top hat, a frock coat, black waistcoat with a cravat. Side whiskers are essentials for the old chap. For ACT II, a long ankle-length nightshirt covered by plaid dressing-gown and topped by a woolly hat.

Sopwith: dowdy black dress, with grubby apron and small hat with a single flower on it, to denote her lower station in life.

Spurgeon: leather coat and cap. Goggles, gloves and gaiters (or leggings), a smart moustache. White shirt with bow tie under coat.

MADE AND PRINTED IN GREAT BRITAIN BY
LATIMER TREND & COMPANY LTD PLYMOUTH

MADE IN ENGLAND